HOPE

for a

SEASON

**EVERYDAY LITURGY *for the*
WEARY *and the* ORDINARY**

PETE BOWELL

PRAISE FOR HOPE FOR A SEASON

There are many books to read if you want to learn, if you want to be challenged, if you want to be entertained. It is the rare book, however, that speaks with such an authentic voice that you forget you are reading a book. The best books aren't books at all—they are friends. In *Hope for a Season*, you'll find that friend in author Pete Bowell. With winsome humor, honest vulnerability, and gentle wisdom, *Hope for a Season* delivers on that promise—story and truth that bring hope for the season, wherever that season finds you.

— NICOLE UNICE, PASTOR AND AUTHOR OF SEVERAL BOOKS ON SPIRITUAL FORMATION, INCLUDING *NOT WHAT I SIGNED UP FOR*. PODCAST HOST OF "HOW TO STUDY THE BIBLE"

Thoughtful and impactful! I love Pete's ability to stay Bible-based in a way that is still accessible to us all so the truth can pierce our hearts. In this devotional, you'll see scripture delivered in a thoroughly authentic way so that it can do more than impress our minds; it can transform us from the inside. This has quickly become a part of my morning routine with the Lord!

— BRANDON SAMUEL, SENIOR PASTOR, THE CHAPEL, RICHMOND, VIRGINIA

Hope for a Season's storytelling is a breath of fresh air. This is not a stagnant devotional but one that constantly reminds us of a God who is kind, dynamic, and ever-present. Bowell navigates the complexities of belief with unwavering honesty, urging us to confront our humanity and embrace a faith that is authentic and true.

— KATIE NIELSEN, HOPE STUDENTS LEAD PASTOR, 1EQ9 ACCREDITED ENNEAGRAM PRACTITIONER

I have worked in close partnership and friendship with Pete Bowell for more than 30 years. Pete lives in and through the Scriptures. He reads the Bible, sits with its content, and prays and journals about it. He's also the most gifted person I have ever known in connecting with people. I'm excited that he has now put many of his reflections in writing. In this book of devotional content, you'll experience Pete's precise insights from decades of important ministry at the intersection of God's love and our humanity.

— **DAVID DWIGHT**, SENIOR PASTOR, HOPE CHURCH, RICHMOND, VIRGINIA. CO-AUTHOR, *START HERE*

A few years ago, I began the practice of pausing in the middle of my work to notice how Jesus was present with me in the moments of my day. Pete's book will become part of that pause. He so beautifully uses scripture and story to remind the reader that you are not alone and that the uncomfortable, broken, messy seasons are exactly the places Jesus does his best work. These short readings inject hope into my soul and allow me to take a deep breath of grace.

— **NINA EDWARDS**, SENIOR DIRECTOR, NATIONAL TRAINING, YOUTH FOR CHRIST USA. CO-AUTHOR, *THREE STORY BIBLE*

Pete Bowell has always been a steady rock for the "one step forward, two steps back" crowd. You know, all of us. The folks who regularly feel like they're hanging on for dear life, who sometimes wish more than anything that they could be living someone else's life. Pete, admittedly a bit cranky without his morning coffee himself, has titled this new devotional *Hope for a Season*, but I'm here to tell you that it's really hope for all seasons.

— **TOM ALLEN**, AUTHOR, *ROLL WITH IT: ENCOUNTERING GRACE, GRINS, GRIDLOCK AND GOD IN EVERYDAY LIFE*

These thoughtful encouragements for navigating life's daily ups and downs are written with the honest humility that is Pete—overflowing from the heart.

— **Steven K. Smith**, Author, *The Virginia Mysteries*

It's been said that you can't lead people to where you haven't been yourself. In *Hope for a Season*, Pete Bowell doesn't merely relay theological concepts about Jesus; he draws from the well of his own profound relationship with Him. Through this devotional, Pete invites us on a behind-the-scenes tour of his life, welcoming us onto his front porch and guiding us through the valleys and mountaintops of his faith journey. It is in these sacred spaces that he illuminates God's generous invitation to our souls. Come, take a seat on the front porch with Pete, and discover hope.

— **Wes Peterson**, Ph.D., Executive Pastor, Hope Church, Richmond, Virginia. Chairman of World Outreach Evangelical Presbyterian Church

Published by Find Life Media
12445 Patterson Avenue
Richmond, Virginia 23238

Book cover design by ebooklaunch.com

Graphics by Jonathan Bowell

Scripture quotations marked (NIV) are taken from the Holy Bible, *New International Version®, NIV®*. Copyright © 1973, 1978, 1984 by Biblica, Inc.™ Used by permission of Zondervan. All rights reserved worldwide.

Scripture quotations marked (MSG) are taken from *THE MESSAGE.* Copyright © 1993, 1994, 1995. Used by permission of NavPress Publishing Group.

Scripture quotations marked (NASB) are taken from the NEW AMERICAN STANDARD BIBLE®, Copyright © 1960, 1962, 1963, 1968, 1971, 1972, 1973, 1975, 1977, 1995 by The Lockman Foundation. Used by permission.

Scripture quotations marked (ESV) are taken from the ESV® Bible (The Holy Bible, English Standard Version®), ©2001 by Crossway, a publishing ministry of Good News Publishers. Used by permission. All rights reserved.

Scripture quotations marked (NKJV) are taken from the New King James Version®. Copyright © 1982 by Thomas Nelson. Used by permission. All rights reserved.

Scripture quotations marked (NLT) are taken from the *Holy Bible*, New Living Translation, copyright © 1996, 2004, 2015 by Tyndale House Foundation. Used by permission of Tyndale House Publishers, Inc., Carol Stream, Illinois 60188. All rights reserved.

Scripture quotations marked (KJV) are taken from the KING JAMES VERSION (KJV): KING JAMES VERSION, public domain.

Scripture quotations marked (CSB) have been taken from the Christian Standard Bible®, Copyright© 2017 by Holman Bible Publishers. Used by permission. Christian Standard Bible® and CSB® are federally registered trademarks of Holman Bible Publishers.

Hardcover ISBN: 978-1-964919-00-3

CONTENTS

HOPE
for a
SEASON

HOW TO READ THIS DEVOTIONAL

Our friend Google tells us that it takes 90 days to build a new rhythm. I like to think of that as a season. Setting new goals and sticking with them for 90 days seems like a realistic target in our distractible world. Building a sustainable life of faith is important in your workplace, your school, or even on the playground with your kids.

The purpose of *Hope for a Season* is to lead us to the rock that is higher than I. Thus, God's word is central in these devotionals. The Bible is not indifferent to the decisions we need to make or the stories that make up our lives. The book of Hebrews explains it this way:

For the word of God is alive and active. Sharper than any double-edged sword, it penetrates even to dividing soul and spirit, joints and marrow; it judges the thoughts and attitudes of the heart. Hebrews 4:12 (NIV)

When a spirit of discouragement begins to weigh you down, I pray that *Hope for a Season* will remind you that you're not alone. My ultimate hope is that God's word would penetrate the places where your soul may be hiding and bring you back into the light again.

Never let any devotional replace God's word in your life. In my quiet time on the front porch of my home, I always begin with prayer and then open the Bible to spend time with one of my friends: Matthew, Mark, Luke, or John. If I don't know what to pray, I look to a Psalm for a word of comfort or lament.

For the perfectionists among us: Don't worry if you miss a day. *Hope for a Season* is not dependent on a specific calendar date. You can always pick up where you left off the next day. For some of us, it might take two seasons to read this book!

At the back of this devotional are five unique spoken words or writings for both Advent and Easter. Depending on the season you're reading in, you can take time to fix your eyes on the manger or the empty tomb during the last week of Advent or Holy week.

Finally, our Christian faith is not meant to be a lone-ranger faith. If you find something meaningful in this devotional, share it with a friend. The Bible says to encourage one another daily as long as it is called today. And today just might be the perfect day.

In this world you will have trouble. But take heart! I have overcome the world. – Jesus

Love In Christ,

Pete

INTRODUCTION

The writer of Hebrews explains faith as confidence in what we hope for and assurance about what we do not see. But if faith also means walking on water, I'm hanging on for dear life in the boat. This devotional tries to be honest about our everyday experiences as we live out our faith. I love story, and I'm familiar with mistakes. I love the water, but in stormy weather, I prefer unsinkable safety.

This 90-day devotional combines all of it. So much of what I've written here comes from the experiences and stories that make up my life and the lives of the people in our church. Sometimes, I'll say to our community of believers and those who want to believe, "Faith is getting up tomorrow and doing another day." Said another way, we don't have to be exact in our theology or perfect before Jesus shows up. Jesus is with us on our best days and our worst. This devotional is about the courage of honest faith. A faith that helps us to see when we can't see. A faith that works beyond Sunday to just another Monday. Honest faith will ask, "Can someone tell me that I'm not alone in my mess-ups or my make-up?"

I try to capture that in every devotional written here. Some speak of hope despite heartbreaking loss. Some try to make you smile and maybe think that this story describes you. But, in the big picture, I want everyone to know that Jesus is with them even after they say amen. He is with us in our everyday routines. There is hope for you and me, even if we're feeling weary or just plain ordinary.

I once read that the preacher's job is not to come up with some extraordinary new insights. The preacher's job is to remind people of what they already know. I've quoted other authors, pastors, and theologians in this devotional because they've inspired me. Most of them can illuminate a bigger room than I can. Maybe they will inspire you to expand your reading list if you like one of their insights.

My wife, Meg, likes to remind me that Jesus did not ask the apostle Peter on the shores of Galilee if he loved his sheep. Jesus asked Peter, do you love me? Well, this devotional tries to capture both. First and foremost, I love Jesus. But as an extrovert, I love the people, too. The mess-ups, the breakups, the broken, and the blessed. I love Jesus, and I want to feed his sheep. Broken and beautiful sheep like you and like me.

Welcome to *Hope for a Season: Everyday Liturgy for The Weary and the Ordinary*.

ROUTINE

W hat holds you? What is your routine? Every morning, the coffee maker is timed perfectly to start my day. I'm a little cranky without my coffee, and Jesus doesn't need another cranky Christian. So, I take my coffee out to the front porch and sit quietly for a bit before beginning my morning conversation with Jesus. I know this sounds like a utopia for those with little ones who rise at the crack of dawn, but trust me, your day will come.

Our routines are what define us. They keep us going through thick and thin. In the Church, we call this "liturgy." It is our pattern of worship. Our liturgy is our worship, prayer, and creeds. It is what holds us when we feel lost or unsure what to say or sing to God.

I don't know if you know this, but one meaning of liturgy is "the work of the people." Pastor Winn Collier described liturgy this way: "Of course, liturgy isn't just what happens on Sunday. We carry the liturgy with us into our lives. We do this work day after day. We do the work of faith, the work of hope, the work of love."

Our liturgy goes beyond Sunday morning worship. By candlelight, flashlight, or firelight, we keep doing God's work even if the rest of the world feels like giving up.

Micah is a short book in the Old Testament. Micah is called a minor prophet, but there is major truth in what he writes. When I need to be reminded of my work as a follower of Christ, Micah tells me this: *"He has shown you, O mortal, what is good. And what does the Lord require of you? To act justly and to love mercy and to walk humbly with your God"* (Micah 6:8 NIV).

This is our liturgy. This is how we keep showing up for one another. We see every human being as created in the image of God, we forgive others as we have been forgiven, and we look to be the hands and feet of Christ wherever we go.

Our liturgy is not some dull or dusty routine in the church. It's our fireman's carry, lifting people to hope again until they have the strength to stand on their own. Liturgy is living water to our soul, and it matters more than you may know.

ALL DAY LONG

Most mornings, I can climb a mountain. I can give up things that comfort me to find a better comforter. I can go to the Y and actually work out instead of just talking to people. I can be a better man. I'm faster, stronger, and smarter. Most mornings, I'm Superman, until I'm not.

Each day progresses, and soon enough, I'm wearing a bad attitude. I can no longer leap tall buildings in a single bound. I'm grounded and then grieve my lack of ability. How do I fill the gap between my morning aspirations and my afternoon laments?

King David knew his need for God every day and all day. *"Guide me in your truth and teach me, for you are God my savior, and my hope is in you all day long"* (Psalms 25:5 NIV).

The presence of Jesus Christ is real. We don't need to give up halfway up the mountain on Monday or any day of the week. Our hope is not superficial. Our hope is a firm assurance of God's presence that carries us, holds us, and fuels us by grace.

Maybe the end of Psalm 25 was written by David at the end of the day. *"Guard my life and rescue me; do not let me be put to shame, for I take refuge in you. May integrity and uprightness protect me, because my hope, Lord, is in you"* (Psalms 25:20-21).

There are 24 hours in a day. The first two hours in the morning are good for me, but then work begins, and worries rise up in me like Kryptonite. It's a mindset. Take a moment as the day wears on to remind yourself that Jesus is your hope all day long. He will carry us, protect us, and fill every gap with grace.

THE BIGGER STORY

I think many of us have opened the Bible in desperation. We close our eyes, hold the Bible in our hands, and let the good book fall open to a random page. We hope the Holy Spirit will guide our index finger to just the right word for our needs.

Like our bodies, most of the time, the weight shifts to the middle. And the middle of the Bible is right around Psalms or Proverbs. Not a bad place to begin for comfort or advice, but I don't recommend this. Yes, God's word speaks to us in our time of need. Yes, there are times when we might stumble on the right verse for our situation, but the message of God's word is greater than that.

In *The Jesus Storybook Bible*, Sally Lloyd-Jones beckons us to the bigger story. "But the Bible isn't mainly about you and what you should be doing. It's about God and what he has done... There are lots of stories in the Bible, but all the stories are telling one Big Story. The Story of how God loves his children and comes to rescue them. It takes the whole Bible to tell this Story. And at the center of this Story, there is a baby. Every Story in the Bible whispers his name."

Your story may be in a difficult chapter. You may be desperately seeking an answer. But "every Story in the Bible whispers his name."

If you let your Bible fall open to the middle, you might find Psalms 143:8: *"Let the morning bring me word of your unfailing love, for I have put my trust in you"* (NIV). If you flip to the New Testament, you might hear Jesus say, *"Come to me, all you who are weary and burdened, and I will give you rest"* (Matthew 11:28).

From Genesis to Revelation, the Bible is the story of a God who left his throne above to rescue the world he loves. You are a part of that bigger story. You don't need to take a chance by closing your eyes and letting your index finger find the magic verse for you. Every story in the Bible whispers his name.

SHALLOWS

We live in the shallows of this world, but we're called to the deeper things of God. When I scroll from image to image on social media, my brain is like a mouse on a wheel. Moving fast but going nowhere. We are living in the shallows when there is no space in our day to remind us of God's presence instead of our consternation. We live in the shallows when the mode of our relaxation is another drink and not moderation.

John Eldredge, in his book *Resilient,* wrote, "The madness of the world around us, with its incessant carnival of distraction and demand, is designed to keep you in the shallows."

David Dwight, a pastor at Hope Church, said, "We live in a culture where exhaustion and anxieties are frying us." How do we draw strength from the almighty when we're trying to draw living water from the daily grind of our lives? How do we turn our attention from the little "g" god of self to the capital "G" God of peace?

Jesus said, *"The one who believes in Me, as the Scripture said, 'From his innermost being will flow rivers of living water'"* (John 7:38 NASB). This means that somewhere beyond our fleeting thoughts, there is a deeper place where God dwells. So how do we get there? Pay attention. If there is an enemy, he will do anything to keep us distracted from the presence of God that is available to us.

Part of paying attention is to remember there is a deeper place. Listen carefully. Set aside time to be quiet. Shut the door of your office, or take a walk and listen. Pay attention to the promise of living water flowing from a deeper place in your soul. Jesus is there. It only takes a moment.

Draw near to God, and he will draw near to you. Breathe deeply, and remember there is a better life beyond the shallows.

Out of the depths I cry to you, Lord; Lord, hear my voice. Let your ears be attentive to my cry for mercy. Psalms 130:1-2 (NIV)

COMPLICATED

Christian growth is complicated in a broken world where we get little Sabbath rest and read more self-help books than there are selves to help. On our best days, we feel like we're in a good place. But most days, we feel like it's one step forward, two steps back. We like to judge our Christian growth by sinless days and then convince ourselves that two out of three ain't bad. We date our journals, mark the moments, and read another book, but the darkness of sin blots out the light, and we feel broken and not worthy again.

Our savior, Jesus Christ, is sufficient, but too often we try to save ourselves. Dane Ortlund, in his book *Deeper*, suggested we serve a JV Jesus. "We have a domesticated view that, for all its doctrinal precision, has downsized the glory of Christ in our hearts."

When the apostle Paul said, *"I have been crucified with Christ and I no longer live but Christ lives in me,"* he meant that the Christian life is constantly dying to self and living with our eyes fixed on Jesus (Galatians 2:20 NIV).

So the next time sin has darkened your heart and left you with little hope of ever getting it right, remember, it was never about you in the first place. Jesus is savior, Jesus is gracious, and Jesus is king.

I think we have a hard time getting it right. Frustration rises up within us and we end up judging others and judging ourselves. But Jesus knows we are *"poor in spirit"* people (Matthew 5:3).

Keep your eyes on Jesus, and don't let the enemy ever say it's too late for you. We are poor-in-spirit people indeed.

I have been crucified with Christ and I no longer live, but Christ lives in me. The life I now live in the body, I live by faith in the Son of God, who loved me and gave himself for me. Galatians 2:20

FINDING HOME

W hen do you know you're almost there?

Our family travels to midcoast Maine most summers. It's a long trip, but there are markers that tell us we're almost there. That "Welcome to Maine" sign right across the New Hampshire line. The cooler temperatures as we drive towards the coast. The little shack called "Red's Eats" is home to the best lobster roll in Maine.

When do you know you're almost there on your journey? When you're lost, when you feel alone, when something good feels too far away—when do you know you're almost there?

In Luke 15, the prodigal son was lost. He was far from home and wondered if home would welcome him again after a season of rebellion. But then, from a distance, but just close enough to see familiar signs, he saw his father running to him. The prodigal could find his way home from there.

I keep a red leaf from a mountaintop hike in the Maine woods in my old journal. It reminds me of something. From that mountaintop with the small village below and the harbor filled with schooners ready to set sail, I was awakened to a much larger world. On that mountain, my ego was downsized, and my worries began to fade. I could see the bigger picture and find my way home from there.

When we allow others to enter into our world. When we enter into a community with those we love, we can find our way home from there. Participation with others is an essential part of Christianity and gives us the strength to persevere.

From the foot of the cross, we find our tears, our confession, and our need, and find a way to breathe again. The Psalmist said, "*You have collected all my tears in your bottle. You have recorded each one in your book*" (Psalms 56:8 NLT). From the cross, God records our tears but remembers our sins no more. We can find our way home from there.

Does your journey feel long and hard? Is it hard to figure out where you are? God our Father runs to you, the mountains beckon you, and the cross is the place of forgiveness for you. You can find your way home from there.

So he got up and went to his father. But while he was still a long way off, his father saw him and was filled with compassion for him; he ran to his son, threw his arms around him and kissed him. Luke 15:20 (NIV)

SABBATH REST

At the height of the pandemic in 2020, we had nine people living in our three-bedroom, two-bathroom house for almost three months. This was our attempt at quarantining together.

After three days of quarantine, my oldest son wasn't sure if this arrangement was going to work. He was looking for some peace and quiet, which he could have found in his own house. So, he instituted something called "Silencio" on Tuesday nights. After dinner, no TV, no cell phones, no talking, and candles lit in almost every common room. I hid in my room with a book in my hands and tears in my eyes, praying for the pandemic and my children to go away.

Most of us are not very good at Sabbath rest. The book of Hebrews is best known for acknowledging the supremacy of Christ and the "Hall of Fame of faith." But tucked away in chapter four is an exhortation for Sabbath. *"There remains then, a Sabbath-rest for the people of God; for anyone who enters God's rest also rests from their works, just as God did from his"* (Hebrews 4:9-10 NIV).

All of us in the church world know about the Sabbath. But to paraphrase Andy Stanley, Sabbath is the one thing that will change everything. Taking a Sabbath reaches into the deepest part of us and reminds us we are created in the image of God.

So why do we avoid Sabbath? Why is it so hard to take a day, or even 24 minutes, to avoid the iPhone, email, or the sucking sound of social media? Maybe our fear of missing out or not mattering anymore is more important to us than we care to admit. What if taking a Sabbath can actually grow our trust in God instead of our need to be available or make a difference?

There remains a Sabbath rest for the people of God, and it will be good for your soul. Silencio.

DAY
8

THE LORD SEES

I don't want to be misunderstood or labeled as theologically light. But I have this cat. We never wanted a cat, but my brother-in-law and sister gave it to us as a kitten when we moved several years ago. The cat brought some comfort to my daughter, who was entering a different district for high school. My daughter is married now and lives on the other side of town. We still have the cat.

Our cat acts more like a dog. She likes to greet us when we get up in the morning and waits for us to come home after work at the end of the day. But mostly, she seems to be lurking around looking for me. If I'm up late at night watching a ballgame, she kneads my leg with her claws and makes herself comfortable on my lap. She sleeps on my freshly folded laundry before I put it away and even finds some comfort on the top of my computer case. Her name is Bella, and here is what I'm reluctant to admit. I have actually grown fond of her.

For some reason, it seems God has used our cat to remind me that he is always near. Our cat feels like a small Aslan from *The Lion, the Witch, and the Wardrobe,* who reminds the children, "Wrong will be right, when Aslan comes in sight. At the sound of his roar, sorrows will be no more."

Psalm 121 speaks a similar kind of poetry. *"The Lord will keep you from all harm—he will watch over your life; the Lord will watch over your coming and going both now and forevermore."* (Psalms 121:7-8 NIV).

We desperately want to believe that. We want to hear God's voice. We want to know that he is with us or watching over us in the hospital room, classroom, or office cubicle. The world is clamoring for our attention, but our soul needs reassurance that Aslan the lion, who represents Jesus in *The Chronicles of Narnia*, is always near.

We still have our cat. She's no Aslan with a powerful roar, but in some small way, she brings me comfort on the hardest of days.

WHAT WE GIVE AWAY

Nathan is a pastor in South Carolina. I met Nathan when he was in elementary school. He was walking with his parents towards the front doors of the high school where our church gathered in the early days. Nathan and his family were coming for the first time. So, I reached into my pocket, took out a few quarters, placed them in Nathan's hand, and said, "Welcome to Hope!" He smiled, looked up at his parents to make sure it was okay, and never looked back.

Giving gifts seems to be my love language. Over the years, two quarters have become two-dollar bills. Inflation is killing me, but children and their parents are still smiling and finding community in a place called Hope.

There is a lot in our cultural milieu that will wipe a smile from our faces. Gun violence, injustice, and uncertainty about the future. Beyond those, there are the struggles with sin and our own imperfections. We want to smile, but we often think God is looking upon us with a frown.

David Powlison wrote a devotional called *Take Heart*. In it, he said, "You can have joy, even in the midst of continuing imperfection, not just by fighting sin well, but by growing in doing good.

Every single person who makes any progress with persistent sin starts to care for other people."

I think what Powlison meant is if you receive mercy and forgiveness, you want to give it away. I know I am a mess, but I also know that God is looking at me with a smile and not a frown.

I have committed Psalm 103 to memory. It gives me hope when I feel hopeless. *"He does not treat us as our sins deserve or repay us according to our iniquities. For as high as the heavens are above the earth, so great is his love for those who fear him"* (Psalms 103:10-11 NIV).

I want to give money away because it might surprise a young person coming to church for the first time. Maybe it will bring a smile to their face instead of a frown. But mostly, I want people to know how much they are loved.

I have received so much mercy from Jesus, and it's the very best thing any of us can give away.

ONLY THE CROSS

I have walked the Via Dolorosa. It's the street Jesus walked carrying the cross to Golgotha, the place where he was crucified. Via Dolorosa is a Latin phrase that means "the way of suffering." But to call it the "way of suffering" feels like a misnomer for the marketplace this street has become.

This somber procession seems disengaged from the tables lined up outside the shops with prayer shawls, coffee mugs, or small crosses for sale. And if you're thirsty, you can pay a dollar and grab a Coke from a refrigerated cooler along the route.

Jesus was surrounded by people in the marketplace on his tortured journey to the hill where he was crucified, yet he was all alone. When you think of a parade of people, you usually think of a celebration or a victory. But this parade, from all appearances, was a procession of death. Jesus Christ was carrying a cross, being spit upon and mocked, while carrying the weight of the world on his shoulders.

The devil doesn't have the power to defeat Jesus, but he's intent on messing up your journey. Staying in the footsteps of Jesus Christ is not easy, but the steps of Jesus always end in victory.

He was pierced for our transgressions, he was crushed for our iniquities; the punishment that brought us peace was on him, and by his wounds we are healed. (Isaiah 53:5 NIV)

Pastor Douglas Webster wrote, "At the birth of the Son of God, there was brightness at midnight; at the death of the Son of God, there was darkness at noon." Have you ever thought about that? Our sins harden us from receiving God's grace and keep us from the glory of our Father's face. Our sins crush us. Our sins distance us from Jesus. We avoid his gaze. We buy trinkets along the Via Dolorosa as he walks by.

But Jesus keeps pursuing us. He knows we're distracted. He knows our propensity for pleasure or how we seek temporary relief from our disappointment or pain. The gravity of our sin is great, but so was his sacrifice. The cross proclaims he won't count our sins against us.

Never lose sight of it: Christ did not come as a nice guy trying to persuade us back to God. His whole purpose was to leave his throne above to rescue the world he loves. That is the only answer. Only the cross is strong enough to save us from our sins. Only the cross can meet us in our weakness. Only the cross of Christ deals both with the depths of despair and the gravity of our sin. Only the cross.

IN A WORLD OF THICKNESS

I n reading some of the great narratives of the Old Testament, I'm reminded that God calls his people to work when he hears the cries of those in need.

That's why God called Moses. *"I have heard their outcry ... and I will send you"* (Exodus 3:7,10 NASB).

1 Samuel 11 describes the Spirit of God rushing upon King Saul and Saul defending the people of Israel. In Judges 14:6, Samson rescues the people of Israel because the Spirit of God *"rushed upon him"* and enabled him to do it.

So, today, let's remember that God raises his people – including you and me – to respond to the cries of those in need.

God has called you, whether you know it or not, because he has heard the cries of his people. Remember and keep remembering, because the thick air here can make you forget. The busyness of your day can cause you to forget. The distractions of life and work and family can make you forget.

Regardless of how big or small we feel our lives are, this is the core of why we are here: to do justice, to have mercy, and to walk humbly with our God. Not to put ourselves out front, not to place our own needs above everything else. But to walk humbly with our God so he can show us the way.

Some days, we don't need a profound thought or new idea, but instead, a simple reminder of why we're here.

In a world of thickness, it's all too easy to forget.

"Here on the mountain, the air is clear and your mind is clear; as you drop down into Narnia, the air will thicken. Take great care that it does not confuse your mind. And the signs which you have learned here will not look at all as you expect them to look, when you meet them there. That is why it is so important to know them by heart and pay no attention to appearances. Remember the signs and believe the signs. Nothing else matters." – *The Silver Chair* by C.S. Lewis

BLESSING

I f there's one thing I've discerned in ministry, it's the loneliness of people. We can be surrounded by small groups and families, and take restful vacations, but at the end of the day, we can still feel alone in the deeper places of our souls.

I think if we all had x-ray eyes and could see the real condition of people in front of us, we might break down and cry and wonder, "Who will help them? Who will help me?"

But we stay hidden. We have become our own refuge and strength. We're afraid to be known; for whatever reason, we're afraid.

Theologian Dale Bruner tells us that the Sermon on the Mount is actually the Sermon from the Valley. It starts low. It starts where most of us live, if we're honest. The Beatitudes bless us not because of our virtues or as a sign of our success but because of our inadequacies.

Image management tends to be the go-to when our hidden sins keep breaking our hearts, but we're afraid to let others know. It's here we can climb the mountain and look into the eyes of Jesus.

"Blessed are the poor in spirit, for theirs is the kingdom of Heaven"

(Matthew 5:3 NIV). Here, we find grace when groveling. Here, we find the strength to let others know.

I still miss my friend Kin. He was my go-to when I wanted to laugh or vent about my day. "Hey Siri, call Kin," was one of my routines while driving home. *"Blessed are those who mourn, for they will be comforted"* (Matthew 5:4). In this Beatitude, we find the one who was broken for us when our hearts are breaking again.

Does my life make a difference? Does anyone notice me or the little things I do because the bigger things overwhelm me? *"Blessed are the meek, for they will inherit the earth"* (Matthew 5:5). Dale Bruner said, "First and literally the Beatitudes are Jesus' surprisingly countercultural God-bless-yous to people in God-awful situations."

We live in a broken world. If we are investing in it, invest wisely because the world will not invest in you. The things of this world will leave you thirsty for more, and the world doesn't care if you're dying of thirst. *"Blessed are those who hunger and thirst for right-eousness, for they will be filled"* (Matthew 5:6). God wants to help us simply because we need help, not because we're one step closer to spiritual perfection.

The Beatitudes start where most of us live. Start living in the presence of God's mercy and grace. Let the Beatitudes be your prayer go-to's this week. Say them again and again. The one teaching you is looking right at you. Blessed are you.

DIVINE OFFICE

The "Divine Office" is one way to describe prayers throughout the day to sanctify our time with God. I'm not great at it, but I often will stop mid-afternoon to remind myself that my workplace is uniquely the Divine Office. Where have I fallen short? How can I remind myself of God's presence before my last meeting of the day?

Often my afternoon prayers will begin with: "Let me hear your voice this afternoon. Your word of real grace to me and not my own imagination of how your mercy works." I want to be reminded of God's real presence and not try to evoke what I want God to say. Sometimes, it's not new information we need but remembrance.

Psalms 25:5 helps us remember this way: *"Guide me in your truth and teach me, for you are God my Savior, and my hope is in you all day long"* (NIV).

The Divine Office is not for those who are holier than thou. It's for all of us. A reminder that God is with us this morning, this afternoon, and all day long.

ANCIENT PATHS

There is a line in a book of prayers by the Puritans that feels like a cry of desperation. "Keep me, for I cannot keep myself." This prayer rings true to me. Sometimes, I don't do the things I should do. Like keeping a good diet or going to the gym. More often, my life feels like it's spinning out of control. "Lord, keep me, for I cannot keep myself" seems to capture our need in a day of anxious uncertainty.

The Puritan prayer book I keep on my desk feels like an ancient path. Prayers with "Ye Olde English" that ground my soul. These prayers come from a deeper place of candlelight in the 1600s, not distracted by the glow of LEDs. They give us words to say when our own words feel inadequate. There is a weight to these prayers that grounds us.

The dictionary defines a creed as "a set of beliefs or aims that guide someone's actions." So "keep me, for I cannot keep myself" feels like a creed for my soul. It's a sturdy prayer, an honest confession to God who hears my need. The creeds of the Church, like the Apostles' Creed, are the words or prayers the community of faith has said together for over 2,000 years. Reciting a creed or prayer together is like a rescue ship when we feel adrift.

Winn Collier, the author of *Love Big, Be Well*, said this about creeds: "Either we have a creed that is thoughtful and reflective, one we have reached through carefully navigating the interplay of our faith, our community, and our conviction, or we have a creed that is ad-hoc, reactive and no sturdier than our own capricious impulses."

The Lord's Prayer, the prayers of the Puritans, or the creeds we recite together on Sunday mornings join us to the faith of the Church when our own faith feels weak. They have been said throughout history to give us hope in times of fear. They do not come and go like Snapchat messages. They are living water to refill the cisterns of our faith that have sprung a leak in a day of self-sufficiency.

"Lord, keep me, for I cannot keep myself."

I believe in God, the Father Almighty,
maker of heaven and earth;
And in Jesus Christ his only Son, our Lord,
Who was conceived by the Holy Spirit,
born of the Virgin Mary,
suffered under Pontius Pilate,
was crucified, dead and buried;
He descended into hell;
The third day he rose again from the dead.
– From the Apostles' Creed

WAY OUT

W hen life gets stressful, we look for a way out. A mild headache keeps us home. We take a right turn towards the mountains instead of a left towards work. Or when things get really bad, we compose a letter of resignation from life. All of these excuses and impulses feel like a way out, but Jesus keeps showing me a way in.

St. Augustine said to those with a restless soul, "You have made us for yourself, O Lord, and our hearts are restless until they rest in You."

I think my problem, maybe our problem, is a restless heart. We keep believing that if we get just enough rest, land the perfect job, or enjoy just a few days with happy children, then our hearts will be at peace. Our bodies and our souls do require Sabbath, but in this life, there is a moving finish line, and our hearts never seem to find the settled place. Maybe the answer is not the way out but the way in.

Right in the middle of Psalm 84, God says, *"Blessed are those whose strength is in you, whose hearts are set on pilgrimage"* (Psalms 84:5 NIV). A pilgrimage is a journey to a sacred place. A place where we can meet with God and be reminded that everything else fades in the light of his presence.

In looking for a way out, the psalmist reminds me that a restless heart needs to find a way *in*. A way towards Jesus. A way with Jesus. There is mercy, forgiveness, and grace when we come this way. There are deep wells of living water on this journey that Jesus will draw to our lips. So we can rest in the places of rest but also in the places of work.

The way out is actually the way in.

DAY
16

YOU HAVE A SAVIOR

We all have our to-do lists today. We have our plans. We have the normal, predictable routines and tasks that make up the majority of our days. But the moments that define us, the moments that will most likely change us, are the disruptive moments, not the routines.

Routine, over the years, can shape us. People might even use our routines to point to us and say, "Yes, that's the kind of person they are. That's what they do." But it's the disruptive moments that have the potential to change the fabric of who we will become.

So what is our attitude when things don't go as planned? How do we handle the disruptive moments? Do we explain them away? Do we get frustrated? Do we seek emotional outlets to blow off steam? Do we grasp our lives more tightly in an effort to maintain control?

These disruptive moments illuminate the areas of our hearts and lives that need deep healing—the areas that are hidden until those disruptions come along to reveal them. You see, disruptive moments stir up the waters of our souls, and sometimes, when waters are stirred up, you see sediment rise to the surface. Anger. Fear. Unhealthy habits.

But here's what those disruptive moments also do: they point us to our need for a Savior. They remind us that as long as we follow the Lord, we still need Jesus every day.

The shepherds had something out of the ordinary happen to them in Luke chapter 2, and how did they respond? They were filled with fear. But then the angel said to them, *"Do not be afraid. I bring you good news that will cause great joy"* (Luke 2:10 NIV). You've got a Savior.

We've got a Savior too. We're going to get angry this week about something, and we might wonder, "Where did that come from?" We might do something we wish we hadn't. We might see things in ourselves that we wish hadn't risen to the surface—things we aren't proud of.

But when that happens, fear not. We have a Savior.

BEING HUMAN

When we imagine God looking down on us, is it with a look of disappointment?

Pastor Louie Giglio once described a low point in his life as though he were on the edge of a pit, and the two hands that tried to push him into the abyss were insecurity and comparison. We lose ourselves when we forget we're created in the image of God. The light in our eyes dims and there is uncertainty in our steps when we forget to yield to God's unfailing love.

I have an old friend, Paul, who once wrote, *"Do not conform to the pattern of this world"* (Romans 12:2 NIV). You're not smart, good-looking, or athletic because someone says you are. Your life is not a scoreboard where someone gets to measure your worth.

Being called a child of God gives us dignity. He is the one that determines our worth. When the world scars us, he heals us. When the world tells us we're not strong enough, Jesus becomes our strength. When we're told we are not good enough, God is good enough for us.

Our joy in this life will be found in making much of God, not making much of us.

There is a larger purpose for us in the one who fashioned us. This is what it means to Be Human.

So God created mankind in his own image, in the image of God he created them; male and female he created them. Genesis 1:27 (NIV)

GENTLE ANSWER

Have you ever gotten angry at an inanimate object? Something not endowed with a life or a spirit? Have you ever kicked your car because it had a flat tire or hit the dashboard with the palm of your hand because the air conditioning gave out? What's my car supposed to do? Turn on its windshield wipers and shed a few tears?

We live in a time when it's easy to get frustrated and lose our temper. We forget the lunch we packed or left our wallet on the kitchen counter, and now we're running late. Maybe our child is sick and has to stay home from school, and all of our plans have to change. The adage "When life gives you lemons, make lemonade" doesn't work because you've run out of sugar to sweeten its sour taste.

Hebrews 12:15 says this: *"Look after each other so that none of you fails to receive the grace of God. Watch out that no poisonous root of bitterness grows up to trouble you, corrupting many"* (NLT). I take that to mean don't let anger get a foothold in your life when life doesn't satisfy.

Scott Sauls, a pastor in Nashville, Tennessee, wrote a book called *A Gentle Answer*. He said, "While true faith is filled with holy fire, it is a fire meant for refining and healing, as opposed to dividing and destroying. If our faith ignites hurt rather than healing upon the bodies, hearts, and souls of other people—even those who treat us unkindly—then something has gone terribly wrong with our faith."

We need Jesus. How can we keep our hearts soft in a world of hardening position? When Jesus said, *"I am gentle and humble in heart"* (Matthew 11:29 NIV), it was not a statement of strategy to reach people, but the spring of water he offered to thirsty souls. I want to be like Jesus. I want to walk close enough to get the dust of his sandals on my own.

What has broken down in your life recently? Sometimes, those things are not in our control. Your Honda doesn't hate you. Don't let the compiled frustrations of living in a broken world make you inordinately mad at an inanimate object.

Let's take care of the people God has put on our path and keep pressing into the unfailing love of Jesus. Let your faith ignite healing, not hurt.

HUMILITY

The ability to care for others is rooted in the soil of humility.

I have been working in ministry for a long time now, and to be honest, the longer I do this work, the less capable I feel. I have gained experience that can speak to many situations, but I realize that my instincts are not always the right ones. As years have passed, I've become more and more reluctant to think, "Here's the answer!" Indeed, my ability for ministry is rooted in the soil of humility. And what does humility look like?

Humility does not assume. These are assumptions we often make: "This is mine," or "I'm stronger than that," or "I could do better than that." But humility does not assume any of those things.

Humility is teachable. Humility keeps learning. We don't want to grow older and think we have nothing left to learn. When we are teachable, we listen to others, and that's a part of humility as well.

And finally, humility serves. Humility is not in a hurry. It asks, "What can I do?" Humility listens to the Spirit for direction and wisdom rather than rushing in with its own thoughts or expertise.

Oswald Chambers says, "One life wholly devoted to God is of more value to God than one hundred lives simply awakened by His Spirit." Then he goes on to say, "Unless the worker lives a life hidden with Christ in God, he is apt to become an irritating dictator instead of an indwelling disciple."

Many of us are dictators, dictating our desires to individuals and groups. But Jesus never dictates to us in that way. Mostly, when our Lord talked about discipleship, he prefaced it with words like "if." *"If anyone desires to come after me"* (Matthew 16:24 NKJV). The way of Jesus was not forceful or dogmatic.

So, let's pursue the example Jesus set for us and settle our hearts on this simple truth today: Humility does not assume. Humility is teachable. Humility serves.

As a prisoner for the Lord, then, I urge you to live a life worthy of the calling you have received. Be completely humble and gentle; be patient, bearing with one another in love. Ephesians 4:1-2 (NIV)

GENTLE AND HUMBLE

E verything seemed harder during COVID-19. Our Zoom
call connections were spotty. Did we remember the hand
sanitizer and mask before we left home? Did we go to the
grocery store and stand in long lines 6 feet apart?

Then, there were the more serious matters that weighed on our
hearts. A friend or relative on the front lines of health care.
Grandparents who could not hug but only wave hello from the
front lawn or behind screen doors. Sadness and despair hung over
us like a never-ending gray cloud during COVID-19.

Recently, I read something meaningful that pastor Charles
Spurgeon wrote in the 1800s. He said there is only one place in
the four Gospel accounts given to us in Matthew, Mark, Luke,
and John where Jesus tells us about his own heart. *"Take my yoke
upon you and learn from me, for I am gentle and humble in heart,
and you will find rest for your souls. For my yoke is easy and my
burden is light"* (Matthew 11:29-30 NIV).

Jesus is gentle in heart. Author Dane Ortlund wrote, "Jesus is not
trigger-happy. Not harsh, reactionary, easily exasperated... The
posture most natural to him is not a pointed finger but open
arms... If Jesus hosted his own personal website, the most prom-

inent line of the 'About Me' dropdown would read: 'Gentle and Lowly in Heart.'"

Jesus says, "*Take my yoke upon you and learn from me.*" If Jesus is gentle, this means his yoke is not just a little less heavy than the burdens we carry around in this world. It means his yoke is life-giving. The yoke of Jesus is more like a life preserver around us that keeps us afloat rather than a heavy crossbar laid across our bodies. Jesus already took care of that load.

The yoke of Jesus is gentle. The yoke of Jesus is kind. The yoke of Jesus is more likened to grace than law. He is gentle and humble in heart. Jesus will guide us through the rip currents of this life and sweep us up in his tender embrace.

Come to me, all you who are weary and burdened, and I will give you rest. Take my yoke upon you and learn from me, for I am gentle and humble in heart, and you will find rest for your souls. For my yoke is easy and my burden is light. Matthew 11:28-30

THE THRILL OF VICTORY

When I was growing up, there was a television show called "Wide World of Sports." It was ESPN before ESPN. It was on television every Saturday afternoon. The broadcast began with these words by announcer Jim McKay: "Spanning the globe to bring you the constant variety of sports, the thrill of victory, and the agony of defeat."

The words "agony of defeat" were accompanied by a video of a ski jumper losing his balance and falling head-first off a steep ramp. You could hear the groans coming from the living rooms of sports fanatics all over the country.

When facing a difficult season of life, it's easy to lose our balance. It's challenging to soar like eagles when you're just trying to do another day.

Henri Nouwen, a Dutch priest and educator, writes that Jesus understands our failures. He understands our pain and disappointments. No doubt, there were times when he experienced frustration in his humanity about what remained to be accomplished. But his steadfast will for the Father's plan—even when that meant he lost all control of his life and had to be perceived as a complete failure–ensured our salvation.

Sometimes, the enormity of what Christ did makes us wonder, how do we fit into this picture personally? Does he know my story? Does he know about my job loss, my illness, or the struggles in my marriage? Would Christ have died if only for me? The answer is yes.

Jesus knows your story. He knows what it is to feel alone. He knows about the financial worries or the broken relationships. He knows what it is to feel weak in crises, and he even knows the temptations that beset us. Remember, for your sake, for our sake, for the world's sake, Jesus did not give in.

But he was pierced for our transgressions, he was crushed for our iniquities; the punishment that brought us peace was on him, and by his wounds we are healed. Isaiah 53:5 (NIV)

Jesus turns our agony of defeat into the thrill of victory.

DAY
22

SHINE YOUR LIGHT

Said very simply, giving glory to God is to shine our light upon God rather than ourselves. In a sense, we shine our light on God by simply being who we are and telling the story of what he's done in our lives.

There are plenty of days when we don't feel worthy to point others toward God, but even when we are discouraged, we can still give God glory. You see, we don't add to God's glory by being more worthy, by feeling sharp and in control on any given day. We simply shine the light we have on God rather than on ourselves. It's really that simple.

If you have felt like the boundaries in your life are out of control, or it's simply a challenging week, I'd like to pass along words that Jesus said toward the end of his life in the gospel of John:

Now my soul is troubled, and what shall I say? "Father, save me from this hour"? No. it was for this very reason I came to this hour. Father, glorify your name. Then a voice came from heaven, "I have glorified it, and I will glorify it again." John 12:27-28 (NIV)

You see, even in trouble, even in times when we aren't running on all cylinders, God will be glorified, and we are invited to be a part of that. The goal is not to do more, be better, or improve ourselves and the veneer of our lives. The goal is to glorify his name and shine the light on him.

RIGHT WITH GOD

Buzz Lightyear is a toy action figure made famous in the movie *Toy Story*. His catchphrase to prove he could fly was, "To infinity and beyond!" Of course, we all know toy action figures can't really fly. In the real world, this phrase is used as simply an idiom to mean limitless possibilities. It's like saying, "I am going to give 110%. I will go above and beyond what is asked of me."

Can anyone give 110% when 100% is the most of anything? Why do we spend so much of our life trying to get right with God when getting right with God is not about our maximum effort?

The apostle Paul put it this way: *"You see, at just the right time, when we were still powerless, Christ died for the ungodly... For if, while we were God's enemies, we were reconciled to him through the death of his Son, how much more, having been reconciled, shall we be saved through his life!"* (Romans 5:6,10 NIV).

Sometimes, I pray, "Lord, keep saving me." I know, once saved, always saved, but it's my way of saying, "Lord, I need you every day." There is nothing I can do to save myself when I go down the dark road of sin again. Oswald Chambers, in his devotional *My Utmost for His Highest,* took this to another level.

"And it is not repentance that saves me—repentance is only the sign that I realize what God has done through Christ Jesus. ... Is it my obedience, consecration, and dedication that make me right with God? It is never that! I am made right with God because, prior to all that, Christ died."

The only way we get to infinity and beyond is by embracing the work of Christ on the cross. If we wear a cross around our neck, it says that Jesus has taken my sins upon a tree and saved me completely, unreservedly, and unconditionally. We are the object of God's affection, and the cross of Calvary goes above and beyond what we could ever do. Only Christ can take me to infinity and beyond.

MYSTERY

There is a couple I know whose little girl experienced complications during delivery and, after a difficult diagnosis, was not expected to live beyond a few weeks. They may not know it, but I was one of those in their wider circle who was aware and kept praying with hope for this little one.

I am unsettled by mystery. I don't like murder mysteries. I don't like waiting to find out who committed the crime. I don't like getting lost. I want to know where I am going without the GPS to guide me.

The prophet Isaiah proclaimed these words from God: *"For my thoughts are not your thoughts, neither are your ways my ways"* (Isaiah 55:8 NIV).

Faith is full of mystery. Sometimes, it's difficult or even impossible to explain the ways of God. I want to know the reason for someone's sickness. I want to know why someone I love is suffering so much. There can be heartbreak and mystery beyond all belief while we wait for the thrill of hope to appear. Pastor Ken Gire wrote, "I think we feel if we can somehow connect all the dots in life in some kind of cause-and-effect manner that life can be managed and made safe for us and for those we love."

Life is not a puzzle to be figured out. We don't always know where the pieces fit. But one day we will see. One day, we will see our savior face to face. But until then, what? Ken Gire wrote, "We huddle together in the storm. Wet and shivering, but together. And maybe in the end it will be our huddling in the storm that gives us more comfort than our understanding of the storm."

Faith is full of mystery, but God won't leave us. So, we will find each other. Maybe wet and shivering, but holding one another and praying for another miracle again.

COURAGE

It takes great courage to live, but my life feels routine. I do what most of us do when we grow up. I go to work, pay the bills, raise children, and try to remember that my wife's love language is found in my acts of service and not watching baseball with me.

Where is the courage in routine?

I'm also a pastor. Most of the people I pray for in the church have inspired me and not the other way around. Some of these saints are fighting cancer, and cancer is fighting back. Others grieve over a lost child or the darkness of depression but still find the courage to live another day. Whenever I enter the story of these courageous people, I'm on holy ground.

When God spoke to Joshua, the man who would replace Moses, he said, *"Be strong and courageous."* God didn't say, "You are courageous" or "Get your act together," God said, *"Be courageous."* We are created in his image, and there is *"incomparably great power for us who believe"* (Ephesians 1:19 NIV). Joshua was no slouch. He was a warrior, but after forty years of wandering around in a desert, it may have been easy for him to fall into an ordinary routine and not believe.

There are disappointments, setbacks, or failures in most of our days. These things can reduce our souls to cowering into a corner. We don't need courage hiding in a corner.

The word "courage" seems out of place in the middle of our routines, but if we remember we can *be* courageous, maybe our view of life could be filled with possibilities instead of problems.

Have I not commanded you? Be strong and courageous. Do not be afraid; do not be discouraged, for the Lord your God will be with you wherever you go. Joshua 1:9

BAPTISM

Standing under a cold shower or taking an ice bath is never comfortable. The polar bear plunge is for the few and the proud, but it's not for me. Every summer on the family trip to Maine, our family stands on the pier over the translucent sixty-degree harbor water and jumps in. Vacation in Maine begins with this traditional plunge.

Lately, I've held back, hoping the kids wouldn't notice. My circulation isn't as good as it used to be, and there is potential for a heart attack that could ruin the rest of our vacation. Most likely, I would be buried along with some relatives in the local cemetery. "Here lies dear old Dad; he jumped in the sixty-degree harbor water in his sixties."

It was late one October when I went down to the river with a friend from our church and her family. She was about to revisit the MD Anderson Cancer Center in Houston, Texas, for life-saving surgery, but first, she wanted to be baptized. I told her the water would be cold, but she was okay with that. She wanted to experience her baptism deep in her bones.

Pastor Winn Collier said our baptismal vows speak of new life but speak of death first. "When you go under, you're not getting some light splash to rinse off the dust. No—you drown under those murky waters. Baptism happens to us once, but it prepares us for a lifetime of drowning, a lifetime of being rescued."

Sometimes, diving into a cold body of water will take our breath away. But maybe that's the point. We may find it hard to breathe, but our commitment to Christ means we're ready for this. Our faith prepares us for the deeper waters of life.

In baptism, God's love will hold us. In the end, God's love will raise us up again.

I have been crucified with Christ and I no longer live, but Christ lives in me. The life I now live in the body, I live by faith in the son of God, who loved me and gave himself for me. Galatians 2:20 (NIV)

POWER

Sometimes, I describe faith as "getting up tomorrow and doing another day." I say it because I know how hard it is to live in the world. I say it because I know friends who struggle with depression or disease. How can I give them a word of encouragement to press on?

Lately, though, I have been rethinking this. Is this setting the bar too low?

Paul, in his letter to the Ephesians, said a prayer for people with battle helmets on and securely fastened to their heads. They were living in foxholes just below the surface of life, and this is what he prayed:

"I keep asking that the God of our Lord Jesus Christ, the glorious Father, may give you the Spirit of wisdom and revelation, so that you know him better. I pray that the eyes of your heart may be enlightened in order that you may know the hope to which he has called you, the riches of his glorious inheritance in his holy people, and his incomparably great power for us who believe." Ephesians 1:17-19 (NIV)

Navy Reserve chaplain Greg Brown commented on this verse. "The implication of Paul's prayer and description of this power was that these believers were living below the power available to them. This no doubt showed up in an ability to conquer sin, to have joy in Christ, and to persevere through trials."

So, what is a believer to do? Get up and remember the one we serve. Rely on the one who lives within us. Our faith is not one that says, "Hey, maybe things will get better." Our faith is a strong and hopeful faith.

On our worst days, we persevere through trials. In our sickness or depression, we press on because we know the best is yet to come. In our complacency, we stop complaining and confidently move forward because Jesus has something for us today. We become a light to those living in darkness and a hand of strength to the fallen ones.

Don't let the news of this day, or any day, discourage you. It is time to raise the bar. Faith is more than getting up tomorrow and doing another day. There is incomparable, great power for us who believe.

PRAY AGAIN

Focused prayer has never been easy for me. I go back and forth between making a list and simply being thankful. I suspect God is smiling when I pray. I don't think he's looking for perfection but for my acknowledgment that God is near. The Bible says I am a child of God, not a self-made man with no need for his Father in heaven.

Pastor Ken Gire referred to prayer in *The Weathering Grace of God*. He wrote, "The language of prayer spans the lexicon of human emotion. There are the light vowels of joy and the low gutturals of sorrow."

This seems about right to me. My suffering prayers cry out, "Oh God, please help me," or "Heal this person I love." My joyful prayers can soar on the wings of the dawn. C.S. Lewis said, "We must lay before Him what is in us, not what ought to be in us."

What is important about prayer *is* prayer. It's our spiritual breathing apparatus. It is how we talk to God. When push comes to shove, most of my prayers settle my restlessness and bring me back into the arms of God.

Ken Gire went on to say that when Jesus prayed fervently in the Garden of Gethsemane, "This was no Renaissance painting. This was a real portrait, a portrait of how we pray when the earth beneath our feet begins to quake."

My prayer life will never be perfect, but in all its imperfections, it is what I bring to God. Daily prayer plants another seed that grows in us more intimacy with Jesus. It's not complicated. Prayer is childlike. It cries, it laughs, it suffers, and it soars. It's how I talk to God.

CANDLELIGHT PRAYERS

I wouldn't consider myself a prayer warrior, but I do pray every day. Sometimes, they are simple prayers like, "Oh God help." At other times, my prayers come from the gut. Groans of concern for my children or for those I love.

Despite my best efforts, I get tired of hearing my own prayers, especially when they become a daily "to-do" list for God.

The Valley of Vision is a collection of Puritan prayers primarily from the 1600s and 1700s. There is a strength to these prayers. The language these Puritans used brings me to a deeper place that goes beyond my limited vocabulary. These prayers speak to my soul, thoughtful prayers written by candlelight without the electricity and speed of the 21st century. Often, I will take the time to read one of these prayers in the midst of my busy day to reorient me again.

One of these Puritan prayers is entitled "To Be Fit for God." Some of the lines in this prayer can remind us of our identity through everyday trials. Go ahead and read this section of it, but listen with your heart.

Deliver me from worldly dispositions,
for I am born from above and bound for glory.
...Let me never slumber, never lose my assurance,
never fail to wear armour when passing through enemy land.
Fit me for every scene and circumstance;
Stay my mind upon thee and turn my trials to blessings,
that they may draw out my gratitude and praise as I see their
design and effects.

I don't know what your day will hold for you. But never forget you are born from above and bound for glory. A helpful reminder when your day feels listless or foreboding. Let this prayer written by candlelight burn brightly in your soul.

AN INVITATION

Think about an invitation you've received recently, perhaps to a party, wedding, or neighborhood event. How did you respond?

Did you accept it? ("Yes, I want to go to that one!") Or did you reject it? ("I'm too busy. We have too much going on.") Or did you simply ignore the invitation altogether? ("I'm just not that interested...")

The truth is, all of us will receive an invitation today – an invitation to connect with Jesus. Like all invitations, it will be one that we can joyfully accept, reject out of stress, or ignore completely.

If we accept the invitation of Jesus, our hearts should have a willingness to go whenever he says, "Follow me." If we reject his invitation, most of the time, it's because we feel a little too busy or distracted to enter into what Jesus is offering us. If we ignore his invitation, our hearts are essentially saying, "I'm just not that interested; I've given up being good enough."

What if the sunrise today is an invitation? What if we could accept this day not as an overwhelming checklist of tasks and appointments but as a new opportunity for God to work in our hearts again? What if a person in need who comes our way is an invitation? What if we choose to see those around us not as disruptions or inconveniences but as invitations to love?

And what if our loneliness, our restlessness, and our guilt are all invitations? What if we could choose to go deeper, to open a book, to enter into prayer, and to connect with Jesus in the midst of our ordinary, unspecial moments?

All of us will receive an invitation today. In fact, Jesus is all over the place, in big and small moments alike, holding out a hand and offering each of us an invitation. The challenge for us is this: to keep our eyes and hearts open for what he's offering and to dare to accept his invitation in our lives today.

Look! I stand at the door and knock. If you hear my voice and open the door, I will come in, and we will share a meal together as friends. Revelation 3:20 (NLT)

DAY
31

AMISH BARN

One of the heart-wrenching things I do as a pastor is grieve with a family whose child has died. John Ortberg, in his book *Faith and Doubt,* says "Every child is a testimony to God's desire that the world go on." Later in the same chapter, Ortberg tells us that "Dostoyevsky, who was a believer, wrote that the 'death of a single infant calls into question the existence of God.'" How do we speak into such suffering and pain? We don't. We show up. We stay present. We grieve, we listen, and we only use words when necessary.

This is what I struggled to say at a memorial service for a precious child who never woke up after she was born. "So, we are here this morning to build an Amish barn of faith together around this precious family. We are here to simply be present. We are here to surround them with our love, our support, and our tears."

The Amish are known for their community of faith that comes around to support and surround anyone in their little village when disaster strikes. The raising of an Amish barn is done quickly. They use a simple and repeatable method. The Amish people show up, work hard, and then show up again the next day. The community gathers with food and strong shoulders to support a family in their time of need.

You don't have to live very long to find out that suffering is a part of the world we live in. The apostle Paul was a tentmaker. He knew what it was to experience loss and pain. So, he said this: *"Rejoice with those who rejoice; mourn with those who mourn"* (Romans 12:15 NIV).

When a young child dies. When someone feels like their heart is breaking and they carry this wound alone, there is something we can do. We can show up with whatever simple tools we have and help rebuild a life. The presence of Christ through us can be enough.

Our souls are not meant to endure this uninvited darkness without help. So, we weep with those who weep. We gather together to build an Amish barn of faith and become a refuge and strength for anyone in need.

God doesn't show up after the suffering; he's already there. He's asking us to join him in this sacred place.

ONE OF THOSE DAYS

All of us have had "one of those days." You're running behind, and the car won't start. The kids went to bed late but still got up before the crack of dawn. You bumped your head, you stubbed your toe, and the garbage bag broke.

Why do these things happen? Or, for the martyrs among us, why do these things always happen to us? I tend to be a chronic complainer. But complaining hasn't made things better; it just adds more focus to the common denominator of my misery, the common denominator of me.

We live in a culture of complaint. Who will lead us beside quiet waters and help us shine like stars instead of sulking behind the clouds of complaint?

The apostle Paul tells us to imitate Christ. *"Do everything without grumbling or arguing, so that you may become blameless and pure, 'children of God without fault in a warped and crooked generation.' Then you will shine among them like stars in the sky as you hold firmly to the word of life"* (Philippians 2:14-16 NIV).

The flat tire attached to your axle may not be your fault, but it may be your time. Feeling unrecognized at work may not be your fault, but it may be your time. More significantly, getting sick may not be your fault, but it may be your time.

At the risk of invoking a child-like faith nursery rhyme, maybe we should "let this little light of ours shine." Shine through the cloud of complaint and point to the author and perfecter of our faith who knows our story. To remember God is good even when the garbage bag breaks or everything is breaking badly for you.

Hold firmly to the word of life. He knows about "one of those days," but his love will always remain. "This little light of mine, I'm gonna let it shine."

LOST AND FOUND

Becky found my wallet. She was meandering through the country on a Saturday drive with her husband, Joe, when she spotted a lost brown billfold on the side of the road. Becky, being a good Samaritan, stopped to pick it up to return it to its rightful owner. To her astonishment, she opened it and saw my smiling face on the driver's license looking back at her.

Becky and I work together at a church called HOPE. It's not unusual for me to misplace things, but this felt like a minor miracle to me. What are the chances someone I work with would be driving through my small town and would find my wallet on the side of the road?

In John 6, Jesus spoke of his Father's will. *"And this is the will of him who sent me, that I shall lose none of all those he has given me, but raise them up at the last day"* (John 6:39 NIV).

I have known the Lord for a long time, but there are still times I feel lost. Lost in my uncertainties and insecurities. Lost in my sin and wondering if Jesus can still find me in my own darkness. But despite feeling lost, I am never lost to Jesus. Jesus will never lose us. He will never discard us. He will never forget about us. This is his grace, and this is his love. We are sheep and Jesus is forever our shepherd.

A miracle is defined as a "surprising and welcomed event that is inexplicable by natural or scientific laws." Becky finding my wallet felt like a little miracle to me. In my wallet was my identification, and she returned it to its rightful owner. Jesus will never lose you. He knows you by name. He will find you on the side of the road and won't walk by. Nothing will snatch you out of his hand.

For I have come down from heaven not to do my will but to do the will of him who sent me. And this is the will of him who sent me, that I shall lose none of all those he has given me, but raise them up at the last day. John 6:38-39

GAMES

My wife tells me you have to be settled to play games. I don't like games. For a season she was playing "Wordle" with friends on her phone. In this game, you get six guesses to figure out a randomly selected five-letter word for the day. I could go into more detail, but that feels like I'm playing the game.

As a young boy, I played Monopoly, checkers, or chess, but for now, or at least until the grandchildren get old enough to play, I'm not interested. Perhaps there is something deeper going on in me or in us. Maybe the anxiety of winning is too closely tied to our identity or our need to produce instead of playing for fun. You have to be settled to play games.

"Game" is defined as a form of play or sport played according to rules and decided by skill, strength, or luck. I wonder if Jesus was playful.

On the evening of that first day of the week, when the disciples were together, with the doors locked for fear of the Jewish leaders, Jesus came and stood among them and said, "Peace be with you!" John 20:19 (NIV)

The door was locked but Jesus walked right into the room. I'm not suggesting Jesus was playing a game, but maybe, just maybe, Jesus was having some fun with his closest friends while demonstrating his power over everything.

We live in a world where peace is elusive. Some of us worry too much, and the margins feel too thin to play games. The boundary lines for us have not fallen in pleasant places.

When Jesus walked into that room and showed his disciples his hands and his side, they were overjoyed. Death was defeated, the tomb was empty, and victory was snatched from the jaws of defeat.

Why are we so overwhelmed? Why are we so locked up? Jesus said, *"Peace be with you"* (John 20:21). You have to be settled to play games.

FRIENDS

In 1997, I moved my family from seminary in Boston to Richmond, Virginia. When I went next door to meet my new neighbor, I found out he was good at fixing things.

We first met when he was under his car, working on the muffler. The muffler was not cooperating, so my new friend expressed his frustration with a few choice words not readily found in the Bible. After a string of expletives, he asked me to hand him a different tool from his toolbox. Then he asked me, "What do you do?" I didn't have the heart to tell him I was a pastor.

You see, the first thing I want people to know is that they matter to God. And because they matter to God, they matter to me. There will always be people we meet that are shouldering burdens like a heavy winter coat. They're not sure if they can tell anyone they're just one more disaster from giving up on God. Pastor Winn Collier wrote about this dynamic when he said, "We Christians often feel anguished by—and compelled to swiftly answer—every doubt that any person struggling with faith voices, any challenge a scientist, philosopher, or ethicist presents. We're afraid that these runaway questions will deliver faith a lethal blow if left unchecked."

I didn't know my new neighbor's experience with people of faith or preachers. All I know is that I wanted to give him room to breathe and make a new friend. When the Bible says Jesus was a friend of sinners, I think it means there is a love that gets down underneath our messiness and still loves us. A love that gives people room to breathe and be real.

When life feels unfair, some people question the goodness of God. Good theology is important, but it doesn't always have to be the lead when someone just wants you to listen. It's our loving kindness and humble confession of our own fears that might help a friend recover faith.

After a few choice words, my new neighbor's muffler got fixed. When my neighbor asked me what I did, I told him I was a teacher. Preachers teach, right? Close, but not good enough. So before handing him another tool, I told him I was a pastor.

One December a few years ago, my neighbor and I went fishing for rockfish on the Chesapeake Bay. December can be mild in Virginia, but I swear to you, that day in December was bitter cold. It was one of my least favorite days ever. But it was easier to bear because my neighbor and I can call one another a friend.

UNITY

Sometimes our motor runs too hot. A few years ago, the red oil light on our Toyota came on. My wife insisted there was something wrong with the car. But I've never let a red light on my dash or an empty gas gauge deter me. In fact, running out of gas is an opportunity for spiritual growth.

Depending on our personality, politics is another topic that can overheat our engines. If fear about our future well-being depends on which candidate gets elected, we should pay attention to our warning lights. When we get fired up about a person's politics, we listen a little less and judge a little more. This should grieve us if we get to the point of mistreating another person made in the image of God. Andy Stanley, a pastor in Atlanta, Georgia, asks this question: "Can we disagree politically, love unconditionally, and pray for unity?"

When Jesus was preparing his followers for his sacrifice on the cross, he spoke important words recorded in the Gospel of John. Theologians call this the "Final Discourse." I try to pay attention when someone I love is saying something important before they leave. Sometimes, it's the last things people say that are the things that last. The last words of Jesus written down in John relate to "abiding and unity." This is the prayer of Jesus in John 17:

I have given them the glory you gave me, so they may be one as we are one. I am in them and you are in me. May they experience such perfect unity that the world will know you sent me and that you love them as much as you love me. John 17:22-23 (NLT)

Our division politically can make a message of unity seem naïve. From our bank accounts to our positions on social issues, perfect unity seems impossible. Maybe it's true. Maybe the stakes are too high. But remember, a first-century rabbi from nowhere standing with 12 nobodies said, "*I will build my church, and the gates of Hades will not overcome it*" (Matthew 16:18 NIV). One day, our political parties will be over, and Jesus will still be king, and his church, with its imperfect people, will still be standing.

It didn't take long for that red oil light in my Toyota to prove me wrong. My son was driving the car when the engine overheated and burned up. It broke down on the side of the road, and we sold it for parts.

Sometimes our engines run too hot. We break down and then break down the people who disagree with us. We may not shout and scream, but we harbor malicious intentions in our hearts.

I don't want hurting people to be my final discourse. Can we disagree politically, love unconditionally, and do all we can through the Holy Spirit's power to bring unity?

KINGDOM OF GOD

"T he time has come," he said. "The kingdom of God has come near. Repent and believe the good news!" Mark 1:15 (NIV)

The Gospel of Mark begins in a hurry. There is no genealogy, like in the opening chapters of Matthew. There is no birth narrative, as we see in Luke. There is no "in the beginning" narrative, as we see in John. Mark wants to get to the real beginning as he sees it, with the opening words of Jesus himself.

What does Jesus mean when he says, "The time has come?" I think Jesus may mean that time is up. That's the bad news part. The world as we know it continues to hurt itself and decay away. Even as God's people, we have a hard time waiting, trusting, or giving ourselves fully to Jesus. Like the apostle Peter, we are prone to deny our Lord or keep him on the outside of our hearts looking in.

But here is the good news. The kingdom of God has come near. Despite all of our frailties and doubts, God and his mercy will be in charge of this world. So Jesus says, "repent." We have spent too much time saying we're sorry but still doing the same things. Now

Jesus says, turn around. Turn away from shallowness, selfishness, or calloused hearts.

Frederick Buechner wrote, "We cannot make the kingdom of God happen, but we can put out leaves as it draws near. We can be kind to each other. We can be kind to ourselves. We can drive back the darkness a little. We can make green places within ourselves and among ourselves where God can make his kingdom happen."

The kingdom of God is at hand. Mark says to believe in the gospel. Believe you are loved beyond your wildest dreams. Believe in the power of Jesus and believe in the power that lives within you. Believe the world is thirsty to find living water or someone living in the light. Maybe that someone is you.

The world is hurting. The time is up. But the kingdom of God reaches out to us even as we reach out to one another.

MORE IS CAUGHT THAN TAUGHT

I am still gaining life experience from my wife. The way she opens our home to guests, the way everything is arranged to make people feel welcomed. Her gift is called hospitality. My expertise is making a mess.

I was drinking coffee from my favorite coffee mug on a Saturday morning. I wanted this comfort close to me, so I placed it on the armrest of the porch chair I was sitting in. When reaching for my book, I knocked this prized porcelain mug onto the unyielding patio. It didn't survive. My wife, in her gentle, enlightening way, suggested that this was not a wise thing to do. She could have just said, "I would never rest my coffee mug in such a precarious position."

The way we live our lives is important. If we're not growing in our faith, then those around us have fewer examples by which to live. Everything we read in scripture, every peace we experience in pain, is not meant for us alone. Maybe this is why Jesus taught us to pray, "*Give us this day*," not, "Give *me* this day," my daily bread. We are called to live in community with others we do life with.

My old friend Paul put it this way: *"Even when we are weighed down with troubles, it is for your comfort and salvation! For when we ourselves are comforted, we will certainly comfort you. Then you can patiently endure the same things we suffer"* (2 Corinthians 1:6 NLT).

Counselor David Powlison expounds on this. "Ultimately everything we learn, even a small increment of wisdom or comforts, becomes something to give away."

Jesus is making us into people who move into the world with what the world needs. When we spend time with Jesus. When we are given such an incredible gift of grace and new mercy every morning, let's give it away. If you have felt a bit dry lately, wondering if Jesus is working in the world, maybe he's inviting you into his work.

Don't leave God's word in a comfortable place, only convenient for you. Maybe it's not the wise thing to do.

GLORY

What do you want to be when you grow up? What was your childhood thought or dream? Pediatrician, truck driver, basketball player, or a rock 'n' roll singer?

But Stephen, full of the Holy Spirit, looked up to heaven and saw the glory of God, and Jesus standing at the right hand of God. Acts 7:55 (NIV)

Stephen cared for the poor and powerless. In the Catholic church, Stephen is known as the patron saint of bricklayers and stonemasons. I like that Stephen got his hands dirty.

My desire, my heart for you, is to let everything else fade and live in view of God's glory. We all have a job description. We all have work to do, but let's live and work for the glory of God.

The Greek word for "glory" is "doxa." It means "praise." We give all praise to God in our work. We are a living doxology to our community. The Hebrew word for "glory" is "kavod." It means "importance, weight, glory, respect, and honor."

Devotional writer Oswald Chambers said, "Get to the end of yourself where you can do nothing, but where he does everything." Chambers is not talking about glory here, but I think he helps us see what living for God's glory might look like. You are not the most important person in the room. You do not carry all the weight, God does. Live for the glory of God.

When you have those days when life feels like a grit-and-grind undertaking, let the sunshine in. Lift your head and live for the glory of God.

What do you want to do when you grow up? Well, I've grown up now, and I want to live for the glory of God.

Let the glory of the Lord endure forever; let the Lord be glad in His works... I will sing to the Lord as long as I live; I will sing praise to my God while I have my being. Psalms 104:31, 33 (NASB1995)

Glory.

LOVE DOES

Most of us are not as secure in God's love as we wish to be. We may also feel insecure about the love of others. We carry around the fear we may be found out as someone desperately flawed. Can we still be loved by God or by others when others discover we're not the greatest thing since sliced bread or peanut butter and jelly?

In his great prayer for us in Ephesians 3, the apostle Paul says we are rooted and established in love. Psalm 33 insists the earth is full of God's unfailing love. Pastor Winn Collier says this means the dirt on which we walk, the very ground holding us up every day of our lives, pulses with God's love. God's love is really big. It restrains us when we're running towards ruin and holds us after we fall. His love knows we are flawed human beings who are tempted daily and struggle with our faith.

So, the next time you say something you regret, the next time you wonder if God's love is big enough to hold you, it is. God's love is more than feelings; it is our firm foundation. It's the ground we walk on.

During the COVID pandemic of 2020, my dad called me. He was almost 87. My mother had died in 2017, so my dad felt alone.

He called to say he would like to come to town to watch my son's backyard wedding. It was a time of social distancing and trying to keep the older population in our country safe from an unknown disease. I didn't know if this was a good idea. As I was stumbling with my words, my 25-year-old daughter took the phone from my hand and said, "Poppa, you are welcome here. We will have a chair for you at a safe distance and make sure you don't hug too many people." That is the boldness of my big-hearted daughter.

Dad wasn't able to wrap his arms around his family that weekend, but God's love was big enough to hold all of us. As Bob Goff likes to say, "Love does." Love does at a small backyard wedding or even when we're less than our best. God's love is the ground we walk on and the kindness we need.

And I pray that you, being rooted and established in love, may have power, together with all the Lord's holy people, to grasp how wide and long and high and deep is the love of Christ, and to know this love that surpasses knowledge—that you may be filled to the measure of all the fullness of God. Ephesians 3:17-19 (NIV)

THE METER MAN

Do you ever expect condemnation but get grace instead? I was sitting on the second deck of my in-laws' home at the beach when I heard someone say from down below, "Is anyone there?" I almost didn't get up.

I like to stay hidden when I take study leave. Or, more honestly, I like to stay hidden until I get my act together. Once again, I was entering confessions of imperfections in my journal. But perhaps a divine presence nudged me to lean over the rail of the second deck and greet this meter man. He had a kind face and a warm countenance. We spoke briefly about the weather and the fact that both of us are still pursuing work and life despite our advancing years. He ended our conversation with a smile and said, "Finish well."

Now, I don't know if this man shared a common faith with me, but it sure felt like he did. In fact, I got up from my chair to glance out the window at the front of the house to see if I could catch him before he left. I would have thanked him for his kindness and told him that no matter what struggles he was facing in his life, I could still see a light within him. I would have told him he was grace to me on that summer day.

Do you ever expect condemnation but get grace instead? The writer of Hebrews tells us we can *"approach God's throne of grace with confidence, so that we may receive mercy and find grace to help us in our time of need"* (Hebrews 4:16 NIV).

As those who believe or want to believe, our insecurities or worries whisper to us on a daily basis. But on this warm summer day, God reminded me that he does not treat us as our sins deserve or repay us according to our iniquities. Our God sits on a throne of grace, not condemnation. Approach it with confidence. It took the meter man to remind me of that.

WHAT WE LOVE

We love Starbucks or the local coffee shop that's unique to us. We love our ice cream or freshly baked chocolate chip cookies. We love a good glass of wine or watching a great show on our favorite streaming service. We love a quiet morning or a brilliant sunset with hues of red, orange, or pink. We love sleeping in our own bed or getting a good deal.

We love a lot of things, but if we considered the merciful love of God, maybe we would right-size our loves.

You see, I'm addicted to the things I love. They give me some comfort. There's nothing wrong with enjoying the things in life if they're in line behind God's love for us. Saint Augustine once said, "Love God, and do whatever you please." Maybe this means that it's not wrong to enjoy the things God has graciously given us, but first, love God.

I have a friend who once said, "I have a 'dumb-ass' that rises up in me and says or does something stupid every day." Sorry for the irreverence, but that kind of sounds right to me. My cold brew or chocolate chip cookie is only a temporary distraction when I sin and try to hide my shame from others. The things I love may taste great, but they are less filling.

Saint Augustine lived a long time ago, but I think he gets it. This is his full quote: "Love God and do whatever you please: for the soul trained in love to God will do nothing to offend the One who is Beloved."

Jesus is beloved to me. Psalm 103 says, *"He does not treat us as our sins deserve or repay us according to our iniquities. For as high as the heavens are above the earth, so great is his love for those who fear him"* (Psalms 103:10-11 NIV).

I love a lot of things, but they pale in comparison to God's love for me. Oh, how I desire that my desires and affections would be first for God alone. I think it's time for us to right-size our loves. Bless the Lord oh my soul, for he has been good to me. Love God and do as you please, indeed.

THE GREAT BEFORE

How has today been for you? How do you feel about what's happened so far? Was yesterday a momentum builder for today?

You see, how we assess our days is often based on our current feelings or what we've accomplished. We could be having a great day, but then one little mishap throws everything off—maybe we experience car trouble, maybe we've had a hard conversation, or maybe we've misplaced our keys. Does this mean it's a bad day? The truth is, it isn't.

In the final discourse of Jesus in John 15, Jesus encourages his disciples before going to the cross. He says this to them: *"You did not choose me, but I chose you and appointed you so that you might go and bear fruit—fruit that will last—and so that whatever you ask in my name the Father will give you"* (John 15:16 NIV).

So, let's consider what I like to call "The Great Before." Before you were born. Before you came into a relationship with God. Before it crossed your mind that God might be important to you, God singled you out as important. Before it crossed your mind that God was going to be the center of your life, you became the apple of his eye.

As a growing believer, I am most unhealthy when I am preoccupied with *myself* instead of what *God* thinks of me.

So, what does all this really mean for us today? It means that we can have a good day. We don't have to live out of our feelings; rather, we can live out of the deeper reservoir of dignity and design. We can consider "The Great Before."

I don't know what your day will be like today. I don't know if your car will break down. If you'll be injured or if you'll get bad news. But whatever happens, remember "The Great Before." *You did not choose me, but I chose you.*

ONE KING

Everyone has a kingdom, and it starts when we're very young. It starts with the 2-year-old who says, "Mine!" It happens in the teenage years when the sign on the door says, "Keep out." It happens in the places we call our man caves or in the living room chair we call our own.

I have a best friend who visits our home from out of town a few times a year. He gets up before the sun rises, which means the coffee I prepared the night before is almost gone when I get up. My friend invades my coffee kingdom. He looks at me with a smile and offers a word of thanks for my hospitality. I reply with a heartfelt, "You're welcome," and then ask, "How long can you stay?"

In his book *Eternity Is Now in Session*, John Ortberg tells us that Dallas Willard defines kingdom as "the range of your effective will." Think about that. My kingdom is wherever my will or my way is done. But Jesus said there is also a kingdom called the *"Kingdom of Heaven."* It is the range of God's effective will. It is wherever God's will is done.

That is why Jesus taught us to pray, Lord, make "up there" come down here. Maybe you've heard it said this way, *"Thy kingdom come. Thy will be done in earth, as it is in heaven"* (Matthew 6:10 KJV).

And what is kingdom work? Every time you pray for someone in need, it's kingdom work. Every time you give to the poor, it's kingdom work. Every time you humble yourself to lift someone else up, it's kingdom work. Every time you bring peace, it's kingdom work. Every time your need for coffee is a distant second to kindness, it's kingdom work.

And then, one day, when we enter into the kingdom of Heaven, we will not be surprised because we have already seen it on earth. Don't miss the kingdom moments.

"You are a king, then!" said Pilate. John 18:37 (NIV)

HOLY INTERFERER

I wonder if the core of so many of our struggles comes down to authority. Who is in control? Who is writing the script of our lives? This struggle starts at an early age. "I can do it all by myself. You're not the boss of me!"

I think I know more than my doctor because I Googled my diagnosis and researched a better treatment plan. I'm running late to this meeting, but it's okay because I worked hard yesterday, and I deserve a break. You're not the boss of me!

What authority did Herod have when Jesus was born in the manger? What authority did Pilate have before Jesus went to the cross? John Stott remarked they both sought to destroy Jesus. That it was envy and a threat to their authority that led them to hand Jesus over.

Stott continued by asking, "I wonder if many of us have done the same? We resent his intrusions into our privacy ... his expectation of our obedience. Why can't he mind his own business ... and leave us alone? ... So we too perceive him as a threatening rival, who disturbs our peace, upsets our status quo, undermines our authority and diminishes our self-respect. We too want to get rid of him."

But Jesus says, *"I am the good shepherd. The good shepherd lays down his life for the sheep. The hired hand is not the shepherd and does not own the sheep. So when he sees the wolf coming, he abandons the sheep and runs away. Then the wolf attacks the flock and scatters it. The man runs away because he is a hired hand and cares nothing for the sheep"* (John 10:11-13 NIV).

Jesus is not a hired hand. Jesus is the Holy Interferer. He loves us too much to leave us alone. And just at the right time, while we were still sinners, Christ died for us. *"I lay my life down for the sheep ... No one takes it from me, but I lay it down on my own accord"* (John 10:14,18).

What a surprise! It's not just Holy interference; it's indescribable love.

CHILDREN

Nothing melts my heart more than my grandson greeting me with "Hi, Poppy" and taking me by the hand to show me his latest Lego creation.

After Jesus rose from the grave, he traveled to the shores of Galilee to greet his disciples again. Galilee is approximately 100 miles from Jerusalem. I wonder if Jesus walked all that way or if he just appeared. Do you ever wonder what your resurrected bodies and abilities will be like? This is not the point, but it's kind of fun to think about. Let's get back to the water's edge.

The boys were out fishing. They were taking up their previous occupation after their dream died. Listen to the gospel of John tell the story.

Just as day was breaking, Jesus stood on the shore; yet the disciples did not know that it was Jesus. Jesus said to them, "Children, do you have any fish?" They answered him, "No." He said to them, "Cast the net on the right side of the boat, and you will find some." So they cast it, and now they were not able to haul it in, because of the quantity of fish. John 21:4-6 (ESV)

One commentary says this about the word "children" in this verse: "A number of translations have 'friends' [in place of 'children'], which is to forsake the original." In my rudimentary understanding of Greek, the translators got it right. The same word John used for "children" in this passage is also found in 1 John 3:1 (NIV):

See what great love the Father has lavished on us, that we should be called children of God! And that is what we are!

Sometimes, I think there are too many adults in the room. We position ourselves, hide our insecurities, go to war, and let go of God's big hand. Jesus loves you. You are called a child of God, for that is what you are. Jesus does not look at you with disdain but with affection. When we fall, he picks us up. When we weep, he feels our pain.

Jesus called out to his disciples on the sea of Galilee, *"Children, do you have any fish?"* I think he's still calling us children today. We can trust him. We can let him carry us when the rocky terrain is too hard to navigate. We can be free from fear when Jesus is near.

Let your heart come alive, you are a son or daughter of God. "Hi, Poppy!" It's time to reach out your hand.

GOOD FOR ME

When someone has the ability to travel at will to sandy beaches and tropical sun, my wife likes to say, "Good for them." My less-than-humble reply is usually, "What about good for me?"

The routines of this life can wear and tear at our souls. The urge to get away is a common expression when everyday life feels more like drudgery than delight. But what if this is all there is? But what about me?

Jesus calls us to himself. One day, after another hard teaching, Jesus said to his disciples, *"You do not want to leave too, do you?"* Simon Peter answered him, *"Lord, to whom shall we go? You have the words of eternal life. We have come to believe and to know that you are the Holy One of God"* (John 6:67-69 NIV).

Whenever I dream of a different life, whenever I want to abandon my real life for a beach umbrella, these words have been weirdly comforting to me. Where else can I go, Lord? You have the words of eternal life.

Our bodies need rest. Our souls need to slow down. We have to find the rhythm of Sabbath in the routines of life. But don't let getting away to some tropical place be the answer for our complaining spirit. Let the rising of the sun be a reminder of God's smile. Let the presence of his Spirit strengthen you. When the Bible says, *"the Word became flesh and blood, and moved into the neighborhood,"* it means life can be found where your life is found (John 1:14 MSG).

Why do we compare our lives to others? This is the life we have been given, and God has something in it for us. If we can find God's presence and joy in the everyday, then maybe the getaway feels less like an escape and more like a gift. Good for them, and good for me.

GRAZING TO GLORY

Some of us are easily distracted. It takes us time to slow down or get away and appreciate what God has for us. My son tells me I have adult ADHD. Some of those symptoms include nervous energy, distraction, and a talkative personality. I interrupted our conversation and told him I was offended. Look, a squirrel!

We live in a world of Sabbath distraction. We hold mini-computers in our hands, and the tyranny of the urgent makes it hard to rest. Culture tells us to look at the blue screens while casting a shadow on our childlike souls.

Psalm 33 tells us that the earth is full of his unfailing love. *"By the word of the Lord the heavens were made, their starry host by the breath of his mouth"* (Psalms 33:6 NIV).

Do we have eyes to see? Are we too busy grazing on the things around us to look up and see the glory of the Lord? We weren't created to be like the animals, brute beasts who react to any stimulus and lower their heads to graze on the grass. We were made to look up. The earth is full of his unfailing love.

Do we have eyes to see?

My son and I have the same kind of wiring. He wrote me a kind note at Christmas and said, "You have taught me more than anyone else in my life about devotional life." Mostly, he saw me spending time with my God on the front porch. But lately, I'm wondering if I should change my morning routine. Maybe a "prayer walk" in the morning while taking in the beauty around me would be better for my active personality.

I wonder if, when God put the moon in place to lift the tide and make the waves, he had us in mind. I bet when God made the mountains and opened the storehouses of heaven to make the rivers flow, he wanted us to look up. To look up and get a glimpse of God's glory.

We are missing so much. There is beauty to be found and glory to be known. The earth is full of his unfailing love.

By the word of the Lord the heavens were made, their starry host by the breath of his mouth. He gathers the waters of the sea into jars; he puts the deep into storehouses. Let all the earth fear the Lord; let all the people of the world revere him. Psalms 33:6-8

BODY IMAGE

At my age, I look better from the neck up. Everything below looks more shapeless than shapely. Some of us are not like that. We work out, eat well, and have 6-pack abs. I, on the other hand, have a one-pack. Is there sugar in syrup? Then yes, please, more syrup.

The apostle Paul wrote, *"Do you not know that your bodies are temples of the Holy Spirit, who is in you, whom you have received from God? You are not your own; you were bought at a price. Therefore honor God with your bodies"* (1 Corinthians 6:19-20 NIV).

I think Paul insinuated that what you unite yourself with, you unite Christ with. If the deepest part of us is united with Christ, then we should honor God with our bodies.

Paul's emphasis is not on membership at Gold's Gym but on Godly living. The context for 1 Corinthians 6 is fleeing from sexual immorality. Paul wants us to flee from those things that stain our souls and break our hearts. Oswald Chambers puts it this way, "Your body is ... the 'Bethlehem' of the Son of God."

Keeping in shape is a worthwhile effort, but guarding your soul is better still. Whatever you unite yourself with, you unite Jesus with. There is grace for those of us who have failed. The one born in the manger is not afraid of our mess. But remember, your body is the Bethlehem of God's son.

We all have more to give for the glory of God. It's time to take care of ourselves, body and soul.

BROTHERS AND SISTERS

Most of us are linked by our circumstances. We live in the same neighborhood. Our children attend the same school. We share a cubicle at work with someone. We remain loyal to a losing football team. Sometimes, we are a fandom founded on irrational hope, followed by inevitable unhappiness.

Sometimes, our circumstances are more serious ones. We sit in a chair next to someone with an IV for chemotherapy. We've lost a son or daughter to addiction or a tragic death. We share the loss of a parent or mentor to old age.

But maybe some of these losses, if we let them, bring other gains. When Jesus was surrounded by the crowds, his mother and brothers were trying to "take charge" of him. Apparently, he was not eating, and his family was concerned. When Jesus was told that his mother and brothers were outside looking for him, the gospel of Mark reports:

Then he looked at those seated in a circle around him and said, "Here are my mother and my brothers! Whoever does God's will is my brother and sister and mother." Mark 3:34-35 (NIV)

Jesus taught us to honor our father and mother, but Jesus also gave us a picture of the Church as our spiritual family.

Recently, I was leading a devotion for the staff at our church. They were seated in a circle, hungry for God's word and the connections that come with serving together on Sundays. We were "linked by our circumstances." As my eyes slowly scanned the circle, I gave voice to the reality in the room. "You are my brother. You are my sister."

We are linked by our circumstances. We may not live in the same neighborhood or share very much in common, but we are the Church. We have loved and we have lost, but mostly we have gained. Brothers and sisters in Christ, linking arms together and never letting go.

THE OLD MAN AT THE DOOR

Sometimes I have a dream. But not any ol' dream. I dream that my children's children will know you can never outrun the love of Jesus Christ. I dream that when they go to sleep at night, no matter how hard the previous day might have been, they will wake up to new mercies only God can give.

More specifically, I dream that in 25 years, an old man with a name tag on a colored lanyard can be a greeter at the door of this church. I dream that children will be running in front of their parents, eager to see their friends or excited to make new ones. I dream they will experience something beautiful and unexpected inside these doors.

I dream that this senior citizen at the door would not say something too out of the ordinary like he is prone to do. Too much good is happening inside these doors to chase the nice new people away.

I hope when people leave after a morning of worship, they will have experienced Sabbath peace. I dream the souls that have been hiding that week, weary from the news of the day, will be renewed in the hope of the gospel.

I hope when people leave the church in the years to come, they will know that a church is not a building but a people that matter to God.

And if they see that golden-ager again as they leave, I hope he seems unremarkable to them. But maybe, just maybe, they might see a gleam in his eye, like he knows something. Like somehow, he has always known, the best is yet to come.

Better is one day in your courts than a thousand elsewhere; I would rather be a doorkeeper in the house of my God than dwell in the tents of the wicked. Psalms 84:10 (NIV)

STRONG AND COURAGEOUS

I wonder if more people put pen to paper during the COVID-19 pandemic.

We have become people who primarily communicate through text or posting stories on social media. But sometimes, an old-fashioned letter can help us slow down and say what we really want to say. So, as a pastor during the pandemic of 2020, I wrote a letter to our congregation to help articulate the hard season it was for all of us. This is what I wrote:

As a pastor, I don't have the expertise to get through this pandemic any better than you. We are all learning during this time of social isolation but being isolated when the Church is all about community is difficult. It puts a big detour sign in our way. All of us are trying to figure out a different path and a different method of doing things. Preaching to an empty auditorium feels like the new normal, but disappointingly so.

We can't wait to be with you again. To be deeply human. To see each other smile and lift the roof off in worship. I don't think any of us will ever take for granted again the person sitting next to us who is singing out of tune. While we're all waiting to see one another face-to-face, I want to share with you a word of encouragement from another letter written long ago.

The apostle Peter begins his first letter to the Church by writing these words: *"To God's elect, exiles scattered."* The Church being "scattered" seems very relevant, doesn't it? But then Peter lifts us to a higher place with his prose inspired by the Holy Spirit.

Praise be to the God and Father of our Lord Jesus Christ! In his great mercy he has given us new birth into a living hope through the resurrection of Jesus Christ from the dead, and into an inheritance that can never perish, spoil or fade. This inheritance is kept in heaven for you, who through faith are shielded by God's power until the coming of the salvation that is ready to be revealed in the last time. In all this you greatly rejoice, though for a little while you may have had to suffer grief in all kinds of trials. 1 Peter 1:3-6 (NIV)

Peter's words, written 2,000 years ago, are timely for us today. I love the little phrase Peter inserts into his letter about being *"shielded by God's power."* Social isolation can cut down the risk of infection during COVID-19, but our souls can still feel heartsick. So, to anyone discouraged out there, to those who miss what it is to be connected and deeply human, your soul is being shielded by God's power.

This week, I received a letter from a friend. He mentioned Joshua, who took God's people into the promised land after Moses died. My friend said, "We're gonna make it through all of this. Take it to the bank." I'm glad my friend chose just the right words when he put his pen to paper. Most of our mailboxes are flooded with bills or junk mail. But a letter from a friend can still change someone's day.

ONENESS IS THE GOAL

Sometimes, in a marriage ceremony, there is a unity candle. After the vows, the bride and the groom take their individual candles, put the two little flames together, and light a larger candle in the middle. The candle in the middle is used to symbolize oneness, or, at least for me, the weight gained as we grow older.

In most relationships, oneness (or weight loss) is difficult to maintain. In a me-centered culture, our candle can become a blowtorch competing for the recognition we think we deserve or the freedom we desire to blaze our own trail.

The apostle Paul speaks of oneness in his letter to the Philippian church. He urges them to have the same love and be one in spirit and of one mind. This means that oneness is the goal. We live in a day and age where the only one that matters is *my* one. My opinion, my politics, or my story. But in marriage, the Bible says that the two should become one.

So, what does that look like? We have the same love. Yes, the same sacrificial love for one another, but also the same love for Jesus, who walks with us through this life. Jesus is never frustrated with you. Our failures or helplessness is why he came. In this journey of faith, there is always Jesus who wants you to bring every anxious moment to him, and the peace of God will guide you.

Be one in spirit. The most important part of us is not our body but our soul. Soul tending is what draws us to God and to one another. So, encourage one another. You will know stuff about one another that no one else knows. You will know one another's deepest hurts and greatest joys. You will know the stuff of the soul. Help each other with the inside stuff. A bad day shouldn't define you. Your love for one another and for God in the deepest places of your life is the core of your being.

Be of one mind. This means you may not always agree, but if oneness is the goal in marriage, sometimes you make sacrifices for the one you love. This takes humility. The same humility that brought Jesus to earth to take on our every sin and to take our every suffering.

Oneness is the goal for marriage, but it's also a homily for living in community as believers. Jesus is the light of the world. He doesn't need our blowtorch to make another way.

Therefore if you have any encouragement from being united with Christ, if any comfort from his love, if any common sharing in the Spirit, if any tenderness and compassion, then make my joy complete by being like-minded, having the same love, being one in spirit and of one mind. Philippians 2:1-2 (NIV)

MEALS

My wife likes cooking shows. "The Lost Kitchen" is one of her favorites. Filmed in the little town of Freedom, Maine, this reality show features farm-to-table specialties. Each course is intentionally prepared to make every meal a meaningful experience. It takes a special invitation to get a seat at this table.

Jesus transformed lives one meal at a time. Matthew the tax collector recorded, *"The Son of Man came eating and drinking, and they say, 'Look at him! A glutton and a drunkard, a friend of tax collectors and sinners!' Yet wisdom is justified by her deeds"* (Matthew 11:19 ESV).

Sometimes the simple things mentioned in scripture are missed. Jesus spent a lot of time around meals, sharing stories, teaching about God, healing the sick, and forgiving the sins of those who needed a second chance. Jesus most likely laughed, loved, and offered the hope of a new life around a meal. In fact, the last act of Jesus before the cross was called the Passover meal. *"This is my body broken for you"* (1 Corinthians 11:24 MSG).

Most of the people Jesus shared a meal with were lost. From Matthew, the tax collector, to the Pharisees, they needed more than food for the stomach, they needed food for the soul. I don't think I have ever considered meals to be medicine, but Jesus did. Meals do more than strengthen our body; they strengthen our inner being.

I think Jesus likes "The Lost Kitchen." But Jesus would not require a special invitation to attend his table. There is a welcome mat on the front porch for tax collectors and sinners like you and me. Never underestimate the power of a meal.

GRATITUDE

A preoccupied soul keeps us from seeing the person in front of us. Have you ever tried to make an appointment to fit a doctor's visit into your busy schedule? What about being on hold for more than a Methuselah minute with one of your service providers? Who picks that "hold" music anyway?

If a real human being eventually picks up, they don't disdain you. You're not enemy number one on their list. Jesus didn't say love your enemies except for the one that puts you on hold.

This person's job may mean that appointment-making or problem-solving may be the only thing they do all day. Usually, I end a phone call with someone who is trying to help me with a word of thanks. I might tell this poor soul on the other end of the line to give themselves a raise and take the rest of the day off. Sometimes, that quip can lead to a brief moment of laughter.

Grumbling and gratitude are both accelerants to the soul. One burns things down, and the other builds up.

The author of Hebrews tells us that encouragement keeps people from being hardened. I wonder if the word "hardened" means "becoming embittered by the unkindness people experience."

Preoccupations can be deadly. The person in front of you or on the phone may wonder if their job will sustain them or have any greater purpose than a paycheck. But maybe, just maybe, you can be a difference-maker today, as long as it's called today.

But encourage one another daily, as long as it is called "Today," so that none of you may be hardened by sin's deceitfulness. Hebrews 3:13 (NIV)

EPIPHANY

n epiphany is "an intuitive grasp of reality through something (such as an event) usually simple and striking."

I do not know about you, but deep within me is a desire to see Jesus. To have a "striking" sense of his presence or to hear his voice. When reading the Gospel of John, I saw something that I hadn't seen before, and it made me smile.

So Peter and the other disciple started for the tomb. Both were running, but the other disciple outran Peter and reached the tomb first. He bent over and looked in at the strips of linen lying there but did not go in. Then Simon Peter came along behind him and went straight into the tomb. John 20:3-6 (NIV)

First of all, it made me smile to imagine this scene. If we can assume the "other disciple" that ran to the tomb was John, then John obviously had a better 100-yard-dash time than Peter. Peter might have been bolder than John (Peter went right into the tomb), but John was the better athlete. I think I would sacrifice some of my impetuous actions for better knees.

One of the sites I have visited in Israel is the tomb where they believe Jesus was placed after the crucifixion. Of all the places I've seen, the tomb seems to be a place of reverence for all who believe. Only two or three people can enter the tomb at one time. The intimacy of it, the possibility of it, can be moving to some people.

John Stott once preached, "I could never myself believe in God, if it were not for the cross... In the real world of pain, how could one worship a God who was immune to it?" Jesus experienced physical death. Jesus knew what it was to suffer. We are not alone in this real world of pain. He is with us even when life feels dark, and the resurrection proves the darkness will never win.

Epiphany. My prayer is that we would know and believe in God's great love for us, even if we don't see.

CONFESSIONS

I'm an expert at backing up a trailer hitched to my truck. It's taken years of practice, but now it's like riding a bike. Except when it's not. Recently, I was in a hurry and backed up too fast. The utility trailer I was towing swung around and put a sizable gash in the side of my truck.

I'm competent at the basics in life, like taking out the trash or making a grilled cheese sandwich, but I'm not an expert at very much. You can put money on it or at least make an insurance claim.

When it comes to relating to others or building a team that works well together, I think our confessions are more important than our competencies. It's good to hone a craft or discover a gift that can be helpful to others, but unity is built with humility.

The book of James has much to say about Christian life and community. *"Therefore confess your sins to each other and pray for each other so that you may be healed"* (James 5:16 NIV).

When someone asks for help or forgiveness, it does something to the human heart. In most cases, it draws us closer to that person and not away. It helps me see that person as one in need with me instead of one ruling over me.

There is no such thing as perfection in the Christian life. What we share most in common with others is our weaknesses, not our strengths. Our resumes can be used to introduce us in a public setting, but it's our confessions that will help us relate.

GRACE EMBRACED

I like to work my way into the good graces of God. I get up early to spend time with Jesus and work overtime to be nice to someone I don't like. Of course, none of this makes sense if we understand God's grace as an undeserved gift.

If you were raised in an environment where most of your mistakes were pointed out as majors instead of minors, it's easy to overcompensate and become a people-pleaser, or for that matter, a God-pleaser. Grace is one of the most talked-about attributes of God, but also one of the most challenging to believe for less-than-perfect people.

The apostle Paul described the implications of grace this way: *"For the grace of God has appeared that offers salvation to all people. It teaches us to say 'No' to ungodliness and worldly passions, and to live self-controlled, upright and godly lives in this present age, while we wait for the blessed hope—the appearing of the glory of our great God and Savior, Jesus Christ"* (Titus 2:11-13 NIV).

How can this be? How can grace teach us to say "No" to ungodliness and worldly passion?

My firstborn is a pastor. He would consider his teenage years and first two years of college his prodigal years. If cleanliness is next to godliness, then the house that he lived in during his early college years was on the doorstep of Hades. Several years ago, I had my son share the pulpit with me on a Sunday morning. I asked him what changed his life. He said, "Dad, it was grace, and grace has a name, and that name is Jesus." I will never forget that.

The prophet Isaiah said, *"The punishment that brought us peace was on him, and by his wounds we are healed"* (Isaiah 53:5). That sounds like an Old Testament definition of grace to me. There's nothing I can do to work my way into the good graces of God. The work was already done on a wooden cross.

When we are forgiven despite our faults, when we're loved when we feel unlovable, it does something inside of us. It breaks down our need to defend ourselves and raises our hands in surrender.

I'm motivated to please the one who needs nothing from me but runs towards me and puts his best robe on me. His grace saved me, his grace sustains me, his grace teaches me. Embrace grace.

OVERCOMERS

What makes a home feel like home? My wife and I have dear friends in Colorado. They love Jesus, and they love people. On New Year's Day, they wanted to sit in the hot tub on the back deck. It was 12 degrees outside, but that didn't matter. Friendship, with a warm drink in hand, can render ineffective any chill in the air.

One day, the disciples of Jesus came to him on the Mount of Olives and asked, *"What will be the sign of your coming?"* Jesus responded, in part, *"Because of the increase of wickedness, the love of most will grow cold"* (Matthew 24:3,12 NIV).

We live in a world that has grown contentious. It's difficult to find friends or warmth among those who may disagree with you. So, what makes a home feel like home? Where can we find love when there is a chill in the air?

Our Colorado friends have been long-suffering. Nancy's husband died after a long battle with ALS. Nina, her sister, shared in the loss, and later, they grieved the death of their father, all in a brief span of time.

Suffering can break you or embitter you. Nancy and Nina have decided to keep opening their home. They don't pretend grief doesn't exist, but hardship has softened their hearts towards others and not hardened it. They couldn't believe in God if it were not for the cross. They know Christ is with them in their suffering, so they will remain with others in theirs.

The cold winds of culture keep blowing. The love of many is growing cold. But one family in Colorado says, "Not yet, Lord." There is room for one more in our hearts and one more in our home.

SHOWING UP

One of the most underrated talents in life is just showing up. I don't have to feel something for God to work.

There are Sundays when the last thing I feel like doing is standing up to give a sermon. My insecurities or inadequacies have gotten the best of me. Will my words make a difference? Will people sense that my own relationship with God feels distant? Do I even deserve to proclaim truth from this pulpit? But when I show up, stand up, and speak up, all the promises of God become "yes" in Jesus Christ, and I get to say amen.

The book of Mark tells the story of a desperate father seeking healing for his son. His son had suffered from childhood. Life for this father and son had been a grit-and-grind undertaking. The father cried, *"'But if you can do anything, take pity on us and help us.' 'If you can?' said Jesus. 'Everything is possible for one who believes.' Immediately the boy's father exclaimed, 'I do believe; help me overcome my unbelief!'"* (Mark 9:22-24 NIV).

We do believe. We have faith, but is it enough faith for God to work? This kind of mindset is dangerously close to works-righteousness. Have we done enough, have we believed enough for God to bless us, heal us, or make us right?

Our faith is far from perfect. We are constantly getting out of the boat and sinking beneath the waves. But if we keep holding our hands out in humility, if we are genuine in our belief but with the desire for more, God will meet us in that place. Greater faith is not earned. It is a gift from God.

One of the most underrated talents in life is just showing up. We do believe, help us overcome our unbelief.

THE GAP

There will always be a gap between who we are and who we want to be. For some of us, the chasm is so wide that giving up feels more realistic than growing up. Jesus says, *"Be holy because I am holy,"* but most of us are living in a self-made hole beneath the ground (1 Peter 1:16 NIV). It's a long way up from there.

Part of the problem in closing this gap is our own effort to "do better next time." I keep a prayer journal, and every time I've fallen, I date my journal and begin counting the days of unsullied living. I'm lucky to make it beyond three days.

The apostle Paul wrote a letter to the Ephesians from prison, a place where the only chance of escape was a jailbreak. Paul reminds us that self-effort is often wasted effort when it comes to the righteous life. Paul writes, *"For it is by grace you have been saved, through faith—and this not from yourselves, it is the gift of God—not by works, so that no one can boast"* (Ephesians 2:8-9).

What if God was working for our good in all things? What if your faith in Jesus Christ meant nothing could disqualify you from his presence in your life? What if our job was not to make the waves but to jump into them?

I have often found that receiving God's grace is a better use of my time than beating myself up and starting all over again. When I remember nothing can separate me from the love of God, the gap gets smaller. Then, I can get back to doing the good works, which God prepared in advance for me to do.

WHEN YOU'RE TIRED

When we're tired and run down, it can take all of our effort to get out of bed in the morning. In those moments, it's grace that wakes us up.

When we're tired, one failure or one sin can ruin our sense of self-worth, no matter what else has been accomplished that day. In those moments, it's grace that gives us hope.

When we're tired, life can feel like a scoreboard that measures our worth by our performance. In those moments, it's grace that replaces grades.

So when we're tired, let's let this be our mantra: Grace got me up. Grace gives me hope. Grace replaces grades.

As you go through your day today, recognize that grace is all around you. Grace is in the shoes that you wear. Grace is in the work that you get to do. Grace is in the relationships you get to have. Grace has a name, and his name is Jesus.

Max Lucado writes, "Grace is everything Jesus. Grace lives because he does, works because he works, matters because he matters. ... To be saved by grace is to be saved by him—not an idea, doctrine, creed, or church membership, but Jesus himself, who will sweep into heaven anyone who so much as gives him the nod."

Even if we're tired today, let's not forget grace. It has appeared to all men. It gets you up. It gives you hope. It replaces any score-board that tries to measure your worth.

Look for it today—it's all around, and it's in the presence of Jesus.

For the grace of God has been revealed, bringing salvation to all people. Titus 2:11 (NLT)

CARE

Life is busy. It's easy not to stop. A cell phone in the hand of someone with a flat tire leads us to the assumption that help is on the way.

We are becoming a society of "caring a little less" people.

When Jesus said, *"The poor you will always have with you,"* he was defending a woman who poured expensive perfume on his head. But then Jesus added, *"And you can help them anytime you want"* (Mark 14:7 NIV). But Jesus, we say, we are short on "anytime." Our schedules are full. We don't like being manipulated, and we don't know who to trust when it comes to those really in need.

Pastor Tim Keller once said, "If Jesus had looked over the lip of heaven and said, 'I'm only going to give my blood to the deserving poor or the ones who didn't contribute to their own mess,' he could have saved himself a trip, because there isn't anyone like that down here."

The word "care" originates from the gothic word "kara," meaning to lament or grieve. When we care, we enter into the pain or grief of others. When we care a little less, we are hiding this great gift of care God gave us. The poor, the broken down, or the hurting will always be with us, but we can choose to help them anytime.

Henri Nouwen once asked, "Why do we keep bypassing each other always on the way to something or someone more important?"

There is vulnerability in care. Sometimes, there is a sacrifice of time or money. The woman who anointed Jesus with perfume cared. Jesus wasn't telling us to ignore the poor or the grieving ones, he was advising us to look around and, when the Spirit leads us, be the one to lavish others with our gifts.

Jesus elevated the dignity of everyone he met. Let's make Jesus famous and do the same.

DAY
64

CALLING

I wonder if calling is less about finding our purpose in life and more about responding to a need we see around us. In seminary, I was taught God's call comes in response to the cries of the people around us.

This is the story of Moses: *"The Israelites groaned in their slavery and cried out, and their cry for help because of their slavery went up to God. God heard their groaning and he remembered his covenant with Abraham, with Isaac and with Jacob. So God looked on the Israelites and was concerned about them...Now Moses was tending the flock of Jethro, his father-in-law"* (Exodus 2:23-25, 3:1 NIV).

What followed was a burning bush, the staff of Moses, and the parting of the Red Sea. God's call came in response to the cries of his people.

Moses was tending sheep. In today's world, he was a farmer, middle manager, school teacher, or maybe more accurately, first responder. Moses didn't know what was before him, but God remembered his covenant and used Moses to lead his people to the promised land.

God has placed you where you are for a reason. It may not make you rich; it may be a place that won't change much, but wherever you are, God may use a burning bush to draw you into someone's cry for help.

Counselor David Powlison equated Ephesians 2, "We are God's handiwork," with our calling.

Powlison said, "So each day, in each situation, you have the opportunity to do and say constructive things that no other human being could do or say. In the loving hands of God, your life is custom-designed and custom-built. And we will all fit together in the end."

God's call for your life often comes in response to the cries of his people. You may not know it at the time, but later, you will understand that God was sending you.

For we are God's handiwork, created in Christ Jesus to do good works, which God prepared in advance for us to do. Ephesians 2:10

DAY
65

NO BIG DEAL

I'm not usually the smartest person in the room, but sometimes I like to think I am. When our fledgling church community was meeting in a school, we transported everything from sound systems to children's toys in a trailer. I became an expert at backing up and taking tight corners with our little tabernacle in tow. Until we found a volunteer.

I dutifully shared my expertise with this rookie. He gently smiled and took it all in as I mimed two hands on a steering wheel, showing him the particulars of towing a trailer. Someone sidled up to me after my demonstration and informed me that Raymond, our volunteer, began his career by driving 18-wheelers, some of the largest trailers known to man.

Why do we need to be a big deal? Why do we lead the conversation with who we know or what we know? Why do most people crave recognition or acclaim?

Maybe we feel missed or not noticed. Maybe we don't feel Jesus is real enough for our real needs. Have you ever stretched out your hand and let an infant grasp one of your fingers with their little hand? *"For you created my inmost being; you knit me together in my mother's womb... Your eyes saw my unformed body; all the days ordained for me were written in your book before one of them came to be"* (Psalms 139:13,16 NIV).

We are precious to God. We are a big deal to the one who put the moon and stars in place. We are a big deal to the one who noticed the blind man who stood by the road and cried. We are a big deal to the one who knew someone touched him even when surrounded by a crowd.

Our security is in Christ. Our identity is in Christ. Our acclaim is in Christ. Back up the trailer and be settled in Christ.

What, then, shall we say in response to these things? If God is for us, who can be against us? Romans 8:31

PRAY ALWAYS

I bought my son a lawnmower. When my oldest son and his wife bought their first home, this was one of my house-warming gifts. But it wasn't easy. Do you know how hard it was to find a lawnmower during the COVID-19 pandemic? Everyone was staying home to do yard work. I was so desperate to find a lawnmower that I started to pray.

You see, I usually save my prayers for the big things. Of course, I always thank God before eating a meal, but generally, there is too much heaviness in the world to ask God's wisdom to pick the fastest line at Chick-fil-A, or for that matter, for a lawnmower.

I found the lawnmower for my son at Lowe's while visiting my father in a smaller town with less competition. I prayed, "Lord, this is my last shot. I really want to get my son a lawnmower." Now, I don't know if the Lord specifically answered my prayer. It could have been that none of the retirees in this retirement town cut their own lawn, but whatever the reason, I was grateful.

Winn Collier once said, "Prayer happens in any place and in any way open to God's presence." I don't think God minds if we pray about the little things if it helps us to practice his presence in everything. In the end, prayer means communion with God, and if praying for a lawnmower acknowledges God is present in every moment, then every prayer is important.

After I bought my son a lawnmower, he sent a video of himself cutting his lawn. He had a big smile on his face. Praying for a lawnmower may seem like a small thing, but it made a connection with my son, and that meant the world to me.

THE SAFEST PLACE TO BE

When there's a snowstorm or a lot of rainfall in a short amount of time, it can create chaos in our lives and communities. The days when nature makes us slow down are a gift, but when the kids are home for several days in a row or the power goes out, that's when they start to be inconvenient.

When things like that happen, especially in nature, we often say things like, "I can't wait until things get back to normal. When can we get back to normal!?"

And that sentiment goes beyond what's happening with the weather. If we go through a challenging time with someone who's ill, or if we're stumbling through a busy, hectic season, we often think, "I just want it to get back to normal."

We talk about things being normal. But often, what we really mean is that we want to be in control. Psalm 29 says, "*Ascribe to the Lord, you heavenly beings, ascribe to the Lord glory and strength. Ascribe to the Lord the glory due his name; worship the Lord in the splendor of his holiness*" (Psalms 29:1-2 NIV).

As believers, we know that we are to live for the glory of God. The word for "glory" in Hebrew is "kavod." It means "weight" or "weightiness." The English word that functions in the same way is "matter." We give weight to that which matters.

If our schedule, our accomplishments, or our worries matter to us more than God, it means that we've given too much weight to those things. If a normal schedule—a week that's in our control—is how we feel good about ourselves, we know that we've probably given it too much weight.

Tim Keller said, "Only if you make God matter the most ... will you have a safe life." Maybe it's time to set aside things to which we have assigned too much weight. Don't let the weight break you. Find your rest in God alone. This is the safest place we can be.

THE RIVER IS LIFE

The line of cars coming through this little village in mid-coast Maine can be unbearable in the summer. It's our family's special place, but don't get curious. This pastor loves his flock but prefers you don't see his unshaven face and holey t-shirts.

There are plenty of charming towns along the Maine coastline, but why is this one bustling with year-round commerce? This special village I'm referring to sits at the headwaters of the Damariscotta River that flows into the sea. The oyster beds and colorful lobster buoys that dot the river like a painting provide a living wage for those who make their life here. The sailboats and trawlers return from the sea following the markers "right on red" to bring people and currency to this little town. The river is life.

The Bible speaks of another river in Psalms 46:4. *"There is a river whose streams make glad the city of God, the holy place where the Most High dwells"* (NIV).

There isn't a river in Jerusalem, only small streams and aqueducts that give life to this arid land. So, what is this river?

On one occasion, Jesus stood up in a crowd and said this: *"'Whoever believes in me, as Scripture has said, rivers of living water will flow from within them.' By this he meant the Spirit, whom those who believed in him were later to receive"* (John 7:38-39).

The river is life. The rivers and streams mentioned in the Bible are often used as an analogy for the Holy Spirit. So often, when our life runs dry, we forsake the spring of living water that God has given us and that flows within us. Jeremiah, the Old Testament prophet, put it this way: *"'My people have committed two sins: They have forsaken me, the spring of living water, and have dug their own cisterns, broken cisterns that cannot hold water'"* (Jeremiah 2:13).

So many of us are perpetually dry. We are unwilling to wait for the Spirit's ministry to us but instead run to emotional outlets that have a dark side and leave us thirsty again.

The river is life. The Lord will send streams your way to refresh you. The patience to wait for it has never failed me. Stop running and stay planted by streams of living water, and you will bear fruit again when the season is right.

By the way, don't try to find me in this special little village in mid-coast Maine. You won't recognize me. I always leave my razor at home.

DIVIDED

"*Return to your rest, my soul, for the Lord has been good to you*" (Psalms 116:7 NIV). It's true, but God's goodness is hard to see when we live with a divided soul. On one hand, we are deeply rooted in faith. On the other hand, we are deeply rooted in the pleasures of this world. The devil doesn't have to bring out the big guns to defeat us in this life. He can simply divide our affections and keep us on the same cul-de-sac.

In Biblical Greek, the word for "worry" is "merimnao." It's the combination of two words, "divide" and "mind." To worry literally means to have a divided mind, or for that matter, a divided soul.

A good friend of mine once said, "You can't lean two ways at the same time. We may try, but we'll end up in some contorted position and grimacing in pain."

Do we trust the Lord to take care of us? Do we trust he will give us our daily bread? Do we trust he's not against us but for us? Do we trust if we seek first the Kingdom of God, that all that we need in this life will be given to us as well?

Trust in the Lord with all your heart and lean not on your own understanding; in all your ways submit to him, and he will make your paths straight. Proverbs 3:5-6

Lord Jesus, show us the ancient path to real life in this modern world. It's time to get out of the cul-de-sac.

BEAUTY

Have you ever seen or climbed Mount Everest, Mount Rainier, or Table Mountain in South Africa? Have you seen Victoria Falls up close or cruised the glaciers of Alaska? Can you describe them?

Mountaineer John Muir said, "No amount of word-making will make a single soul to 'know' these mountains. One day's exposure to these mountains is better than a cartload of books."

I believe there is this entire life of beauty behind things. There is a Mount Everest behind every mundane Monday. There is a Victoria Falls of power and hope behind every prayer for healing. There is a Mount Rainier perspective behind every reconciling act. This encourages me when things feel bleak, uncertain, or difficult.

C.S. Lewis wrote a sermon called "The Weight of Glory." It was written during World War II to give inspiration and the hope of the gospel during a time of great doubt and fear. This is what he said: "The books or the music or the mountains in which we thought beauty was located will betray us if we trust them; it was not in them it only came through them, and what came through them was longing."

Longing for what?

What no eye has seen, no ear has heard, and no human heart has conceived—God has prepared these things for those who love him. 1 Corinthians 2:9 (CSB)

There is this entire life of beauty behind things. Sometimes, we see it on a Sabbath day when we take time to notice things. Sometimes, we only see it for a fleeting moment, like a reflection in a mirror. Sometimes, it takes a whole life to see beauty rise from the ashes of suffering. But every day, a little bit more of Jesus emerges behind the heartbreaks. There is beauty, there is always beauty, and one day we will fully see. One day, exposure to Jesus will be all we need.

SUNSET

W hat is more enjoyable, watching a sunrise or a sunset? I've never been an early riser, so a sunset fits my rhythm. I'm not a meteorologist, but it seems to me a sunset is more vibrant in color and scope. My in-laws live in Virginia Beach. Every evening, a sunset crew sets up chairs and a cooler on a wide stretch of sand to take in the view. Maybe it's just another excuse for happy hour, but I think it's more meaningful than that.

The scribes and poets who wrote the psalms had a great appreciation for God's creation. Psalms 113:3 describes the dawn and the dusk this way. *"From the rising of the sun to the place where it sets, the name of the Lord is to be praised"* (NIV).

We live in unsettled times. People are looking for consistency and meaning when the loudest voices get all the attention. But with every morning and every evening, we're reminded of God's faithfulness. Once in a while, you might even see an Instagram post of a sunrise or sunset with the caption, "God is showing off."

For some of us, the setting sun is foreboding. We don't sleep well at night or fear the darkness. Tish Warren, an Episcopal priest, wrote a book called *Prayer in the Night: For Those Who Work or*

Watch or Weep. She asked, "How can we trust God in the dark?" Warren suggests that God will not expel the darkness but promises to stay near until the sun rises again.

I don't know if you're a sunrise or a sunset person, but with each one, God reminds us that he's near. That even behind the cacophony of voices in our culture, from the rising of the sun to the place where it sets, the name of the Lord is to be praised.

GLORIFY HIS NAME

When the sun rises, I get up and look at the person in the mirror staring back at me. It takes faith after that glance to pull it all together and move on with my day. So, I muster up another day of faith. Faith that Jesus died on a cross and exchanged his sacrifice of love for the shame of my sin. Faith that despite my failures, my heavenly father waits for me. Faith that the sun rises every morning even when my countenance feels like a cloudy day. Faith that the gospel is advancing somewhere or someplace even when I am in full retreat. Faith that I can be Holy Spirit-fed and Holy Spirit-led.

Don't stare at me. It's not my power or godliness that makes me great.

After Peter's divine orthopedic work, healing the man lame from birth, Peter said this:

Fellow Israelites, why does this surprise you? Why do you stare at us as if by our own power or godliness we had made this man walk? The God of Abraham, Isaac and Jacob, the God of our fathers, has glorified his servant Jesus. Acts 3:12-13 (NIV)

Whatever we do, however the kingdom of God advances, this is the work of God, not our own.

Don't stare at me. Because if you do I might just engage that look to feel good about myself or my gifts. After Peter's divine healing, Peter declared, *"It is Jesus' name and the faith that comes through him that has completely healed him, as you can all see"* (Acts 3:16).

Don't stare at me. Forgive us, Lord, for the many ways we have lingered in front of the mirror. It's only Jesus people should see. Glorify his name. Amen.

WHOSE LIFE IS IT, ANYWAY?

I often wish my life was someone else's life. I want the intellect of my good friend in ministry. He might use a word like "mellifluous" to describe the beauty of a song. I can't even pronounce the word. I want to be in shape like my best friend, who gets on the elliptical daily at the YMCA. He works out like his goal is to climb Mount Everest, whereas I can barely climb out of bed. I want the diet of Tom Brady. He was considered the greatest NFL quarterback of all time. His enemy is sugar, but the Bible says the fear of the Lord is sweeter than honey. I'm just trying to be Biblical.

We can learn from others, but our life should not be merely a compilation of everyone else's life. The further we get from God, the more we let our idols become our identity, the more we begin to lose our soul and become discontent with our life as we know it.

Psalm 139 should be our mantra when we feel unsettled. *"I praise You because I am fearfully and wonderfully made; your works are wonderful, I know that full well"* (Psalms 139:14 NIV).

I am not a counselor, but I do a lot of counseling in ministry. Sometimes, I ask questions, but mostly, I just listen. The brokenness people experience in this world breaks my heart. When I am looking for something to say, something to help put the pieces of a fractured life back together, I remind them they are created in the image of God. I remind them their savior also suffered, and I remind them they are fearfully and wonderfully made.

When your soul whispers to you, "Get a life," remember, you already have one. As messy as it might be, it's your life. You probably won't climb Mount Everest or be the greatest of all time, but God will give you enough footholds for another day.

"Mellifluous" means sweet-sounding or having a smooth, rich flow. Look it up, or better yet, look up. You are fearfully and wonderfully made. Awake my soul and sing. You are here on purpose.

HONEST PRAYER

Lord Jesus, my heart longs for you in a dry and weary land where there is no water. Too often, I drink from polluted streams to quench my weary soul. My fragile faith is shaken until you remind me again of your grace. Let your word become active in me today.

Remind me that though I have fallen, I will rise again. Though I sit in darkness, the Lord will be my light.

Remind me that this life I live in the flesh, I live by faith in the son of God, who loved me and gave himself for me.

Remind me that Jesus lifts me out of this slimy pit and steadies me for another day.

Remind me that God's unfailing love endures beyond my shame.

Remind me that your church gathers to worship as imperfect people, but together, we are better than alone.

Remind me that God gives us this day our daily bread.

Remind me of God's incomparably great power for us who believe, and that this power, without fail, is greater than me. Amen.

DAY 75

CHOSEN

I'm pretty choosy. I like medium-rare, not well-done. I like my coffee hot and my beer cold. I like to think my way is the best way and pray for those who disagree with my brilliance.

In short, I have a low tolerance for the imperfections I see in others and don't like it when others see fault in me; I think I'm being misunderstood. In the story of the prodigal son, I'm the one who stayed at home. I smile at the returning brother because that's what I'm supposed to do, but my heart is in a distant, resentful place.

If happiness in our lives is dependent upon the ones deserving our love, then we'll be forever dissatisfied and discouraged.

In John 15, Jesus said, *"You did not choose me, but I chose you and appointed you so that you might go and bear fruit"* (John 15:16 NIV). Fruit-bearing is not easy to do when you are grafted into the weed of discontent rather than the tree of life.

Jesus did not choose me on the basis of my goodness or my likeability. He did not choose me because I am mostly right when it comes to hot coffee or righteous living. He chose me because he loves me. Now, that may sound too simple, but if love were based on my standard for likeability, I would be the last one chosen on the playground of this life.

The fact that Jesus chooses us is so empowering. He forgives all our sins, heals all our diseases, and redeems our life from the pit. Jesus likes us even when what we see looking at us in the mirror is unlikeable. Maybe I should be less choosy because Jesus has chosen me.

DAY
76

ABIDE AND ABOUND

I 've never considered myself the brightest light bulb in the box. I borrow from saints of old to build bridges from ancient truths to contemporary times. I use alliteration or mnemonic devices to guide me and remind me of God's truth when life feels cloudy. It helps me to keep things simple.

What keeps me following the footsteps of Jesus when I'm prone to make my own tracks? It may not work for you, but this alliteration is helpful to me: "Abide and Abound."

In his final days with the disciples, Jesus said, *"Abide in me, and I in you. As the branch cannot bear fruit by itself, unless it abides in the vine, neither can you, unless you abide in me"* (John 15:4 ESV).

Then the apostle Paul exhorted the believers in this way: *"Therefore, my beloved brothers, be steadfast, immovable, always abounding in the work of the Lord, knowing that in the Lord your labor is not in vain"* (1 Corinthians 15:58).

"Abide and Abound." These are the two bookends of the Christian life. They remind us of our calling when one day feels indistinguishable from another.

Do we hydroplane over our spiritual life, or are we a person of honest prayer? Do we name our sins specifically or confess them superficially? Do we express joy and sorrow deeply? Is the Lord our shepherd, and we shall not want? Do we trust Jesus with our heavy load, or do we carry it on our own? Is Jesus with us after we say "amen"? These questions help us "Abide."

Have I discovered the passions God has hard-wired into me? Have I developed my gifts to the fullest? Do I think of my work as Kingdom work and use my gifts to create a picture of this Kingdom for others? Do I see myself as connected to a living body? Do I love others as Christ has loved me? These questions help us "Abound."

I am not the brightest light bulb in the box, but I shine brighter when I "Abide and Abound." Alliterate, and then participate in God's work for you.

LOCKED OUT

W as there ever a time you got locked out and had to break in? Or maybe a time you were locked in but broke out?

A week later his disciples were in the house again, and Thomas was with them. Though the doors were locked, Jesus came and stood among them and said, "Peace be with you!" John 20:26 (NIV)

Though the doors were locked, Jesus came and stood among them and said, *"Peace be with you."* Jesus said, *"Peace be with you"* a lot. Jesus said this three times in John 20. When things felt most unsettled, when the future was uncertain, Jesus said, *"Peace be with you."*

Where are the locked places in your life? The places of uncertainty or worry? Sometimes, the locked place for me isn't worry, but the place where I feel my perspective is the right one or my way is the right one, but there still isn't peace. Sometimes, my way matters too much to me.

Jesus will not leave you alone. He will walk right into those locked places of worry or stubbornness and say, *"Peace be with you."*

The word for "peace" in Greek is "eirene." The root of the word "eirene" is "eiro." It means "to join into a whole." When Jesus says, *"Peace be with you,"* maybe he is saying, I want you to be whole again.

Jesus will not leave us alone. He goes through our locked doors and says, *"Eirene. Peace be with you."*

SIMPLE FAITH

I work at a church, where Mother's Day is one of the busiest Sundays of the year. A gift for my wife on Mother's Day was "occasionally" overlooked. "Occasionally" is defined as "infrequent intervals." I will use it in a sentence for you: "Very *occasionally,* this condition can result in death."

Mother's Day Sunday is important to most families, so as a pastor, I would leave early for church while my wife was at home scrambling to get our children out the door. I will never forget the Mother's Day when I ran to 7-Eleven after worship to get my wife an inspirational book from the carousel stand and a rose from the bucket in the check-out line. I have been making up for that Sunday ever since.

Now we plant a tree. My wife loves the outdoors. So we decided on that fateful day to wait on a Mother's Day gift until after we got home and plant something beautiful to mark the occasion. We have planted magnolia trees, cherry trees, apple trees, and other various plants in our yard to enjoy beyond Mother's Day.

We prepare the soil, plant our arbor, and enjoy the fruit of our labor for years to come. The funny thing about trees is they just grow. The rain nourishes them, the sun stretches their branches to the sky, and the roots just keep getting deeper.

There are so many days when we wonder if our faith is where it should be. We don't feel we have made enough effort. Or the tree may grow, but it doesn't appear to have any fruit. It could be there's a disease or disobedience in our life we need to deal with, but Jesus says a little faith can do hard things, one mountain at a time.

David Powlison once said, "Broken humans can shine with the simplicity of faith." I like that. Your faith is enough. Plant the seed, stay near to God, care for those closest to you, and watch your faith grow.

GROW

T here will be a time in your life when you will give up the dream of being a superstar. You may have a season of some acclaim, but outwardly, you only have so much time. My dream was to be the next Larry Bird. For the younger readers among us, Bird was not an ornithologist but a Hall of Fame basketball player.

The apostle Paul has some encouraging words for us in this regard: *"Therefore we do not lose heart. Though outwardly we are wasting away, yet inwardly we are being renewed day by day. For our light and momentary troubles are achieving for us an eternal glory that far outweighs them all. So we fix our eyes not on what is seen, but on what is unseen, since what is seen is temporary, but what is unseen is eternal"* (2 Corinthians 4:16-18 NIV).

Our growth as followers of Christ does not follow the pattern of the world. In my life, this is the growth equation: Sin, Suffering, Mercy Seat, and finally, Deeper Roots.

My growth in Christ is not dependent on my physical strength, my book knowledge, or the latest preacher podcast. Simple ol' me matters to Jesus. The Bible says he is interceding for me on this perilous journey called life. He wants me to look beyond my circumstances and take me to a higher place.

Jesus knows that every failure, sin, or suffering can either end me or grow me. Dane Ortlund writes in his book *Deeper,* "We will not grow in Christ if we view his presence and favor as a ticking clock, ready for an alarm to go off once we fail him enough."

The mercy seat of God in the Old Testament was a place of God's glory. It represented his presence with God's people and his forgiveness of their sins.

When you are ready to give up the idea of the Hall of Fame Christian, go ahead and take a mercy seat. Outwardly, you are wasting away, but inwardly, God is growing you to a deeper place. A place where he is working in your every circumstance, both happy and hard, to see his glory and find his peace.

THE CHILD

There can be a child in all of us. An innocence that marches to the beat of a different drum. A child can find joy in marching through the mud where others just see the mess. A child can pick up the white dandelion and blow it to the wind, while others are winded by worry. A child may fear the darkness but will always find courage when holding the hand of a friend or sneaking into their parents' room to sleep at night.

There is a child in all of us. A shared common language to be needed, loved, and known. We need someone to hold us and tell us it will be okay when the tears begin to flow. We need someone to help us find the wonder in the simple things that most of us miss.

When Jesus walked on this earth, he called a little child to him and had him stand among the crowd. Jesus told his disciples: *"Truly I tell you, unless you change and become like little children, you will never enter the kingdom of heaven. Therefore, whoever takes the lowly position of this child is the greatest in the kingdom of heaven"* (Matthew 18:3-4 NIV).

Whenever our church dedicates or baptizes a child, we ask the big people in our community to raise their hands as an expression of support for the family. I often challenge those who raise their hands to get down on a knee and say hello to the little ones in our midst. I don't want any one of us to miss the least of these. I don't want anyone to miss the kingdom work that can be done by getting on their knees.

Our world is complicated. The acrimonious political climate can make it difficult to have a rational conversation. The stresses many of us feel are squeezing the child right out of us. Maybe it's time to catch a firefly, build a snowman, or pick up a dandelion and blow it into the wind. It won't fix everything, but maybe getting small is better than getting bigger and trying to solve everything on our own.

Trust Jesus with childlike faith, and remember his arms are strong enough to carry us home.

NOT FINISHED

Do you ever feel like the Lord is done with you? It's a real and reasonable feeling because you're done with you. Why do my fears still beset me? Why do my addictions or idols always win? Why does our anger at being overlooked or misjudged still simmer in us?

Psalm 103 attests to God's compassion for us. *"As a father has compassion on his children, so the Lord has compassion on those who fear him; for he knows how we are formed, he remembers that we are dust"* (Psalms 103:13-14 NIV).

God's expectations of us are realistic. In fact, those expectations are the most real things there are. He chooses to use these worn-out and weary vessels. God knows we've skinned our knees from this grit-and-grind undertaking of faith. The apostle Paul wrote, *"But God chose the foolish things of the world to shame the wise; God chose the weak things of the world to shame the strong"* (1 Corinthians 1:27).

God will always get the glory, not us. The world has molded us to consider power and position to be priorities. To work hard or accomplish something is not sin, but don't be conformed to the patterns and expectations of the world. In the quiet place or the confessional place, do you know where your strength comes from? Do you know who gets the glory and who gives the gifts?

If God gets the glory, we get the good. We can stand in every fire that faces us. We can rise after falling, skinned knees and all, if the "good" means God is with us.

REBELLION

Rebellion seems to be in my DNA. If the sign says "Keep Out," I'm wondering what's inside. If the box says, "Do Not Touch, these cookies are for the gospel class," I still might take one to assist the teacher in teaching grace.

On a more serious note, when someone tells me "no," or things don't go my way, I take it personally. I smile on the outside, but a negative narrative is swirling around on the inside. I want to avoid the easy answer here. This kind of rebellion is not an easy fix. It requires a lifetime of repentance and remembering God is patient with us. I don't mean to say God's patience is a fix for taking the cookies from the cookie jar. But remembering God's patience with us does cultivate a grateful heart.

I don't know if I've ever thought about this before, but our rebellion began when Adam and Eve took the apple from the tree. Later, the apostle Peter tells us that Jesus *"bore our sins in his body on the tree, that we might die to sin and live to righteousness. By his wounds you have been healed"* (1 Peter 2:24 ESV).

The apple of rebellion in Genesis came from a tree thousands of years before Christ. But Jesus demonstrated his great love for us by dying on the timber that made a cross. The tree of my rebellion, deeply rooted in me, can be repurposed to be a cross that saves me.

Oh, what love. Oh, what patience. Oh, what kindness. Our rebellion will never make us happy. Our rebellion is rooted in our selfishness and pride and leaves others in its destructive wake. Jesus does not want to live there. Jesus, in his tender care, keeps beckoning us to follow him.

The best for us is not behind the locked door or cookies from the cookie jar. Our rebellion is a dead end. The cross is the power for us who believe. From the cross flows forgiveness and life to the full. By his wounds, you have been healed.

SEASONS

My wife enjoys changing the decor over our fireplace mantle to reflect each unique season. Every Christmas, there are large pinecones and little silver trees lined up to create a mini winter wonderland. She also believes if we were to move to a new state or country, it would take the four seasons of winter, spring, summer, and fall to find our footing.

All of this is encouraging to me. When I'm stuck in a season of suffering, I trust a new season will come. It helps me to persevere when I am yearning for the warmth of spring.

The apostle Peter knew all about suffering. His denial of Christ led to a new season of boldness, even when imprisoned and persecuted for this faith. He wrote, *"Resist him, standing firm in the faith, because you know that the family of believers throughout the world is undergoing the same kind of sufferings. And the God of all grace, who called you to his eternal glory in Christ, after you have suffered a little while, will himself restore you and make you strong, firm and steadfast"* (1 Peter 5:9-10 NIV).

This idea of anticipating a new season sounds hopeful, but it doesn't change things for the reader who feels the chill of winter that keeps them stuck or their tires spinning in the same place. Of course, for those who love the winter, maybe your misery is the heat and humidity of summer. What do you do while you wait for the season to change?

We are not alone in our suffering. Stay near to the family of believers. Take a walk together with a hot drink in your hands or maybe a cold one if you're in the dog days of summer. Whatever the season, the mantle will always change, and you will find your footing again.

THE CHURCH OPENS

I once heard the story of a dog that got loose on a high school football field during a game. Someone's canine was sprinting around like a scrambling quarterback refusing to be caught. At one point, people in the stands started whistling for the dog to come to them. This poor pet started running around in circles, not knowing where to go.

There are a lot of voices yelling in our culture right now. In my line of work, there are religious pundits and church experts whistling about the future of the Church. "Too many people are watching church online." "The Church needs to be more experiential and less theological." "The younger generation is looking for life in other places." It's enough to make you run around in circles.

Pastor Winn Collier said this: "We *are* the church. We're incompetent at most endeavors, but the Spirit has gifted us with divine energy to live into a simple and straightforward vocation. Gathered at Jesus's table, we feast on true life and then disperse into our run-of-the-mill lives as witnesses to the kingdom of this Jesus who loves the whole world. The world needs *more* of who we are, not less."

Jesus calls us *"the light of the world"* (Matthew 5:14 NIV). There are moments in history when the Church needs to shine brighter and not shrink back. To say in the current moment, "This is how the love of Christ compels us."

The writer of Hebrews says we are not to forsake *"meeting together ... but encouraging one another—and all the more as you see the Day* [the promise of eternal life] *approaching"* (Hebrews 10:25). The Church will never fade into individualism but will always be called into the power of a community to love others wherever that may be.

The commentators and the critics will always have something to say, and sometimes, it's important to listen and improve. But the Church isn't going anywhere. The Church is stronger than any pandemic or social unrest. It's the body of Christ, and I will never lose hope in it.

DESCENDING GRACE

Growing up, my dad required my brother and me to clean out the garage every Saturday morning. We would empty it out, sweep, and then return the garage decor to its proper place after we were done. The only thing we looked forward to during this weekend chore was backing the car out of the garage before we were legal to drive.

I grew up learning that my good standing required something from me. There's nothing wrong with hard work or a chore, but don't let that translate into your relationship with God. We don't earn God's love by being good. That's called "works righteousness." Works righteousness is the opposite of good news. God doesn't love us because we're good. God loves us because he is good and full of grace.

The apostle Paul writes, *"But by the grace of God I am what I am, and his grace to me was not without effect. No, I worked harder than all of them—yet not I, but the grace of God that was with me"* (1 Corinthians 15:10 NIV).

Paul knew he could not earn God's love. In fact, Paul called himself the chief of sinners. Paul found out he was loved by God and then was compelled to do gospel work.

John Piper puts grace this way: "Grace is not only God's disposition to do good for us when we don't deserve it. It is an actual power from God that acts and makes good things happen in us and for us." In other words, grace is still operating whether you or I feel close to God or not.

Grace is strong when you are weak.

Grace gives you the words when you have none to give.

Grace gives you compassion to care for others you struggle with.

Grace is the waterfall in you that never dries up.

Grace is inexhaustible when you are exhausted.

This is descending grace. It falls on us before our life is perfect and before the garage is picked up.

IT CERTAINLY IS OUR TIME

The story of Tabitha in the Bible is hugely significant because she was raised from the dead. But what strikes me about her story is what this woman did for people. The passage in Acts 9 says that she made clothing for the widows, who were likely disenfranchised. It says that she gave to the church. She cared for people, and she served them.

Tabitha was likely a woman of means, but she didn't shrug and say, "Well, those widows—it's their fault that they haven't picked themselves up by their bootstraps and gotten better." She didn't ask questions. She didn't make judgments. She simply saw a need and did what she could to help.

John Ortberg, in his book *I'd Like You More If You Were More Like Me*, quoted Barbara Williams Skinner, a faith leader for racial reconciliation: "It may not be your fault, but it certainly is your time."

Ortberg picked up on Skinner's idea, writing, "It's not your fault that some people have no place to sleep tonight. It's not your fault that children are going to bed hungry. It's not your fault that orphans have no home, or that sick people have no medicine. It's not your fault, but you can do something... Who knows but that you have come to your position for such a time as this? It may not be your fault, but it certainly is your time."

Today, we come across people with all kinds of needs. And those people may ask things of us. It's easy to get busy, to become "compassion weary," or to ask, "Whose fault is this anyway?"

But perhaps that is the wrong question. It might not be our fault, but it certainly can be our time.

The homeless person with the cardboard sign on the street corner may not be your fault, but it may be your time. Feeling unrecognized at work may not be your fault, but it may be your time. More significantly, getting sick may not be your fault, but it may be your time.

In Joppa there was a disciple named Tabitha (in Greek her name is Dorcas); she was always doing good and helping the poor. About that time she became sick and died, and her body was washed and placed in an upstairs room. Lydda was near Joppa; so when the disciples heard that Peter was in Lydda, they sent two men to him and urged him, "Please come at once!" Peter went with them, and when he arrived he was taken upstairs to the room. All the widows stood around him, crying and showing him the robes and other clothing that Dorcas had made while she was still with them. Peter sent them all out of the room; then he got down on his knees and prayed. Turning toward the dead woman, he said, "Tabitha, get up." She opened her eyes, and seeing Peter she sat up. Acts 9:36-40 (NIV)

DOUBT

I wonder what it would be like to be a twin. Could you sense when your twin was going through a tough time? Would you intuitively know what your twin was going to say before they said it?

My wife wouldn't have liked knowing there were two of me in our early days of dating. I think she felt I was "too much." Too much energy, too much crazy, too good-looking. I actually made that last one up. Mostly, I'm grateful for my wife's grace to take a chance on me in the days of my youth.

After the resurrection, Thomas, who is called "the twin" in the New Testament, wasn't in the room when Jesus first appeared to the disciples. Pastor Frederick Buechner once said, "If you want to know who the other twin is, I can tell you. I am the other twin." In a world full of cynicism and uncertainty about the future, doubting Thomas could have been my twin, too.

Thomas never did touch Jesus with his finger or reach out his hand to confirm his resurrection. It seems Thomas had finally seen Jesus with the eyes of his heart, and there was nothing more he could say or do.

Sometimes, it feels hard to believe when we see hurt around us or in us. We want more proof of God's love or existence. But in the long run, it's not our eyes that will see Jesus but our hearts.

We will see him when we are moved by the spirit to care for a friend. We will see him in the hospital room when we sense his comforting presence in the midst of our pain. We will see him when we come to the end of ourselves and say, "God, only you can be my refuge and strength."

Sometimes, I'm the other twin. Maybe you are, too. But every time the doubt creeps in, every time the discouragement keeps you in the darkness, there is some sunrise or saint sent from the heart of God to open the eyes of our hearts again. And we can say with Thomas, "*My Lord and my God!*" (John 20:28 NIV).

THE BIRTH OF JESUS

My granddaughter was born in the month of September. Life was ramping up for another season of ministry when I came by the hospital to see my granddaughter for the first time. I walked into the room without any expectations of being the first one to hold this little one, but my daughter put her into my arms. I sat in a chair and was quiet. I didn't want to let her go. My granddaughter was a gift to me. There was nothing to do in that hospital room but hold her. My soul was quieted, and there was peace.

It's a marvel to me that Jesus came as an infant. That the God of all power was born in humility. The angels said it this way: *"Glory to God in the highest heaven, and on earth peace to those on whom his favor rests"* (Luke 2:14 NIV).

Jesus, born as a child, wants me to know his peace.

Henri Nouwen, a priest, author, and teacher, spoke of Jesus born into our dark world. He said, "When I have no eyes for the small signs of God's presence—the smile of a baby, the carefree play of children, the words of encouragement and gestures of love offered by friends—I will always remain tempted to despair."

It is easy to despair in this world. It's hard to behold the one born in a manger when we are busy beholding ourselves. God knew exactly what he was doing when he came to us as a child. God in the manger. Humility but glory. Vulnerability but power. Jesus can meet our every human condition.

Jesus wants us to know his peace. It starts with our being vulnerable to him as he has been to us. It starts with slowing down, humbling ourselves, and trusting our lives to the one who knows our hurt. I was holding my granddaughter right after she was born, but in reality, she was holding me. Peace on earth.

AFTER AMEN

Focus is not my forte, so for most of my adult life, I've journaled my prayers. Pen-to-paper helps center me when I am tempted to check the score from last night's game or glance at a distracting text from the idol on my desk, otherwise known as my phone. One morning a while ago, I ended my prayer by writing this in my journal: "In Jesus' name...," but instead of writing "amen," I scrawled, "You are with me even after amen."

I'm not sure why that came to me. Maybe unconsciously, when I say "amen," I move on with my day, and I assume Jesus moves on with his day as well. Most mornings, I'm sure Jesus has bigger fish to fry than my prayers for my family's well-being or a blessing for my success.

Episcopal priest Tish Warren said, "We are discipled by nearly every impulse of our culture to believe that the here-and-now is all there is; that the only hope offered for us is found in what we can taste, smell, feel, and see."

For distractible me, the here-and-now Jesus feels more real in my set-aside time for prayer. But Jesus' realness is not determined by my schedule. Is Jesus only real when I decide he is real? Is Jesus disinterested in me when I've failed to be faithful again?

When Moses told Joshua that God would be with him like he was with Moses, he meant it. *"He will not leave you or forsake you"* (Deuteronomy 31:8 ESV). Jesus continues to be present even after we say amen. More importantly, for the sinners among us, the ones distracted by scores and texts and to-dos, the unfailing love of Jesus doesn't fail us even when we've fallen short of the mark again.

Jesus is present with every breath we take. I'm still not sure why I wrote in my journal, "In Jesus' name ... you are with me even after I say amen." But then again, maybe those words were whispered to my soul by Jesus. Maybe the most real thing is not the here-and-now in front of me but my Jesus who remains in me.

And be sure of this: I am with you always, even to the end of the age. Matthew 28:20 (NLT)

DAY
90

NOT MY WILL

I think that when most people think about miracles, they think about physical healing. But what about the miracle of finding joy even in sorrow? What about the miracle of overcoming addictions? What about the miracle of raising kids? (I've got three miracles.) What about the miracle of feeling secure when there's no reason to feel secure? What about the miracle of faith? The kind of faith that prays, "Not my will but yours be done?"

This kind of faith is a thing against all reasonable things to pray when overwhelmed with sorrow. No one seeks suffering in this life, but when it comes, we tend to look for self-help more than a savior.

When Jesus prayed, *"Not my will but yours be done,"* in the garden of Gethsemane, it was a prayer of faith and trust in his Father. Theologian Dale Bruner says that in the garden Jesus taught the Church how to pray one more time. Can the prayer of Jesus become our own?

I wonder if every time Jesus prayed, *"Not my will but yours be done,"* in the garden, the angels began to gather, and the light of heaven got brighter. I wonder if every time Jesus said, *"Not my will but yours be done,"* heaven began to rumble. I wonder if every time Jesus said, *"Not my will but yours be done,"* the earth shook, the rocks split, and everything was about to change forever.

The prophecy in Isaiah 53 about Jesus, made 700 years before Jesus was born, began to be fulfilled in the Garden of Gethsemane when Jesus prayed, *"Not my will but yours be done."*

But he was pierced for our transgressions, he was crushed for our iniquities; the punishment that brought us peace was on him, and by his wounds we are healed. Isaiah 53:5 (NIV)

"Not my will but yours be done" was a massive expression of faith that released the power of heaven and enabled the miracle of our rescue to take hold of us.

In our suffering or uncertainty, we often look for a way out. But the prayer of Jesus in the Garden was our way in. Maybe it can be our prayer as well.

ADVENT

ROOM IN THE INN

*T*he people walking in darkness have seen a great light; on those living in the land of deep darkness a light has dawned. Isaiah 9:2 (NIV)

Advent begins in the dark. Christmas begins in a shepherd's field under a starlit sky in the little town of Bethlehem. Christmas begins with no room in the inn.

No room for the mom who comforts her child in the hospital room. No room for the young couple who can barely make ends meet. No room for the one who feels like this sin was the sin that even God can't forgive. No room for the one suffering in silence behind their smiles, hugs, and things to do.

But this is the surprise of Christmas. The unseen town, the unheard prayer, or even the unseen grief is where God shows up.

The angels first announced, "Christ the Lord," to the night shift. The high and lofty one was made low and helpless. The one who was born in a one-light town remembers us in our low estate. This is the surprise of Christmas.

No one then would have believed that a king was born in a feeding trough. But this was a profoundly human event. God knows us. God sees us. Now we can believe. There is always room in the inn. There is always a crack in the door filled with light.

It's why we light up our homes and light up our world. It's why we open the doors for one another and try to be kind to one another. It's why we look to be a Christmas miracle for someone we see, because we need a miracle too. The miracle that a light can still shine in our darkness.

There is room for us in the inn. There is room for the harassed and the helpless. There is room for the one in need of mercy. There is room for believing unbelievers who need one more miracle to believe again. There is room for the brokenhearted. The manger is where we find one another. His name is Jesus. The one born in the manger can be born in us again.

ADVENT

HOW GOD COMES TO US

H ow will God come to us? Frederick Buechner wrote,
"Those who believe in God can never in a way be sure
of him again. Once they have seen him in a stable, they
can never be sure where he will appear or to what lengths he will
go or to what ludicrous depths of self-humiliation he will descend
in his wild pursuit of humankind."

Buechner goes on to tell us that if the holiness and majesty of God
were present in the manger, then there's nowhere we can hide
from God. No place where we are safe from his power to break in
and recreate the human heart. It's just where he seems most helpless, where he is most strong. It's where we least expect him where
he comes most fully.

"O Magnum Mysterium" is a 7-minute song that whispers to the
soul that Christ has come. It was written in the 1500s as a 6-part
vocal harmony to describe the joy and awe felt by the shepherds in
the manger where Christ was born.

"O Great Mystery" was written to respond to complaints.
Complaints that the religious music of the day was too plain.
People needed a miracle. Joy and awe were in short supply, just as
joy and awe are absent today.

So, if you have a chance, look up "O Magnum Mysterium" on Spotify, Pandora, or whatever service through which your music comes to you. Then close your eyes and listen. When you open your eyes, remember the miracle of the virgin birth and that God is still doing miracles today. Remember that the angels first announced his birth to shepherds, and he can still announce his presence to you.

Imagine the lonely widow, the broken teen, the "happy" family with worldly means but empty souls. Imagine yourself longing for something more, but then God shows up and reminds you that your labor for the Lord is not in vain. Remember that God left his throne to rescue the world he loves, and he is still intervening today.

The light is still showing up. The light shines in the darkness, and the darkness will never win.

ADVENT

MOHAIR SWEATERS

The worst Christmas gift I have ever purchased was a blue mohair sweater for my wife. It looked like a sweater that put its sleeve into an electric socket. For the uninformed, mohair is a soft wool that comes from the hair of an Angora goat. I don't know what an Angora goat looks like, but nobody's wife wants to look like a furry, four-legged animal.

The perfect Christmas gift has never been harder to come by. In a world that increasingly acts like Ebenezer Scrooge, we need the gift of reconciliation, healing, and giving others a second chance. Not a second chance for people to get their act together but a second chance to be a human being who is frail and imperfect.

The only perfect gift the world has ever received was a baby born in a manger and wrapped not in expensive mohair, but in simple strips of cloth to keep him warm. This baby grew up to extend us grace, heal our hurts, and open his arms to receive people who don't believe they deserve a second chance.

In Psalm 56, King David writes that God is for us. *"Record my misery; list my tears on your scroll—are they not in your record? Then my enemies will turn back when I call for help. By this I will know that God is for me"* (Psalms 56:8-9 NIV).

I don't mean to be silly or irreverent, but this child born in a manger did not say "You'd better watch out, you'd better not cry, you'd better not pout, I'm telling you why." In fact, this son of a king doesn't remember our sins but instead records our tears. One day our God will make everything sad become untrue.

Come thou long expected Jesus, born to set thy people free, from our fears and sins release us, let us find our rest in Thee. This song of Christmas is the cry of our souls.

CHRISTMAS HUMILITY

The world could use a dose of humility ... starting with me. I want to be on the cover of *Men's Health* magazine, but the scale in my bathroom and my fragile core have me sitting on my keister for another year's Christmas picture. My son Jonathan calls me the patriarch of the family. I think that means "family founder," but it sounds like a nice way of saying I'm ancient.

I'm writing this during Advent and looking at a nativity scene we've set up in the family room. The word humility comes to mind for me. There is a rawness in the manger. It feels real to me. Like, God knows my life. He knows my efforts and my failures. My joy in holding my grandchildren in my arms but my weakness in wishing I was more. More fit, less sarcastic, and better at spending meaningful time with family.

There is a song called "Away in a Manger" that was written in the nineteenth century. It tells of the humility of Christ's birth. There's always been pride in the human heart, but I think this song was written in a humbler time. The world could use a dose of this humility. Every year our news source blows up with another politician pontificating to get elected. It saddens me to anticipate the shouting, the positioning, and the pride of "our way is the best way." But I wonder if we could be a people of "manger ways." Quiet but persistent in our care for our family, neighbors, and friends.

God is so good. His love is steadfast for me. The apostle Paul tells us that God's son *"did not consider equality with God something to be used to his own advantage; rather, he made himself nothing by taking the very nature of a servant"* (Philippians 2:6-7 NIV).

God knows us; he gets us; he was born helpless in a manger, no crib for a bed. From the very beginning, Jesus was humble in all his ways. A people of manger ways. That sounds just about right to me. There is always a way in the manger for us. A little humility to hold one another up, one hand at a time.

WHERE DOES KINDNESS COME FROM?

Where does kindness come from? It would be easy to cast stones at the American Christmas. The Black Friday sales, the traffic that keeps you home in the comfort of Amazon. The over-indulgence and the under-served, but where does kindness come from? The American Christmas can't help but whisper of something beyond our best efforts to express the light.

And yet, every Christmas, Ebenezer Scrooge seems to show up again. There are more bah humbugs and less hallelujahs. More fears and less fear-nots. Fewer small white paper bags filled with sand and candles to line our streets and illuminate the heart.

The simplicity of such a display rekindles our soul, but so does the wonder in a child's eyes on a tacky lights tour with the inflatable Santa Claus on the roof. So does the Christmas tree in our homes or the candlelight in our windows. It all points to something more. It reminds us of the Dickens story, the possibility of one person's transformation from cruel to kind. Our transformation from alone to loved.

Christmas offers the worn-out and weary a message of hope.

Could it be in the grandeur, in the singing of carols and the greetings of Merry Christmas, there is a whisper of something more to make us whole again?

Could it be that there is something small enough, humble enough, and kind enough to fill us and fan into a flame these smoldering wicks? Could it be in the manger there was light in the darkness, wealth in poverty, and comfort in hardship to recreate the human heart?

Could it be that there is a great promise that comes to us on Christmas Day? Something stronger, braver, and kinder than the world has ever known. The American Christmas can distract us but can't silence the whisper that in the manger, we find one another.

This is where kindness comes from. His name is Jesus. Word became flesh. The one born in the manger has never failed us yet.

THE MEANING OF MIRACLES

What if the "meaning of miracles" had a greater meaning beyond a miracle for me? Do we desire divine intervention without the cross of the divine?

We are poor and needy enough to cry out for a miracle, but most of the time we just negotiate. If we can muster up a bit more faith. If we behave for more than 3 days, God will you do this miracle for me? We're more self-righteous than poor in spirit.

We have things upside down, as if the potter was thought to be the clay.

And what are these miracles we seek? Someone to intervene in our boring routine or to help us in our desperate state. A flash of lightning, the winning ticket, or a chair on the beach to rest our weary souls.

We want a cure for the epidemic of our day. We want our loneliness to go away. We are one step away from holding a cardboard confession on the street corner. "I need help" is the cry of our souls, but we don't want to write it down that way.

We want our prodigals to come home or a child to be cured. We want a love that lasts a lifetime or a marriage to be remade. We want a few more years when the diagnosis is measured in fewer days.

We're looking for divine intervention without the cross of the divine. The prophet Isaiah cried, *"Yet it was the Lord's will to crush him and cause him to suffer, and though the Lord makes his life an offering for sin, he will see his offspring and prolong his days"* (Isaiah 53:10 NIV). Not my will but yours be done.

So, what is this miracle we seek? Frederick Buechner put it this way: "To believe that Christ is risen and alive in the world is to believe that there is no place or person or thing in the world through which we ourselves may not be made more alive by His life."

Maybe the miracle we seek is to be more alive. To be more courageous and more certain that Christ is present with us even if we don't have eyes to see. "Not my will but yours be done" is the prayer that brings Christ closer to me.

We may not articulate it this way, but the miracle we need is the empty grave. We need to know there is more beauty, if not here, then somewhere. More beauty than the world has ever known. We need to know that there was a divine cross that understood our suffering and bears our pain. Not my will, but yours be done.

We need to know that our God is the grave robber beyond the garden tomb. This is the miracle we need, and this is the miracle we get. Jesus is risen. He picks us up from rock bottom and puts us on our feet again. His body and blood shed for me. Not my will but yours be done.

EASTER

THE LAST SUPPER

"Seriously?" Have you ever heard that expression? We've all used it at one time or another. "Seriously?" It tends to be an incredulous statement. "Seriously, you ate the last cookie on the plate?" "Seriously, you turned down the offer for a free weekend at the five-star resort?" "Seriously, you're leaving?"

We don't lack information on the Lord's supper, but the application for our life feels short-lived. We reduce the Lord's supper down to a formal religious habit only to be practiced on special occasions and then forgotten. *Do this in remembrance of me* should ring in our ears whenever the daily grind leaves us broken or poor in spirit.

The word "incredulous" means "an unwillingness to believe something." A skepticism to believe something that is true. I don't want to do this anymore. I don't want to come to the communion table without belief.

Paul Tripp, in *The Journey to the Cross*, speculated, "If all Jesus had done were perform physical healings, then we would still be the spiritual walking dead. If all he had done were confront the false religion of the scribes ... but had not gone on to be the sacrificial Lamb that true religion requires, then we would be doomed. ...

But he *is* the Passover lamb. He *is* the fulfillment of the covenant promises of old. His blood covers and cleanses us."

"Seriously?" Yes, seriously. The death of Jesus Christ on the cross brings his people into a new covenant relationship with God. He is the Passover lamb sacrificed for us. The Lord's table is divine rescue for the poor and needy.

"*Do this in remembrance of me.*" Do not let the familiarity of these words lose their impact. Every time you come to the communion table, there is a powerful act of God on our behalf. He is with you, and you are in Christ. You are a child of God.

And he took bread, gave thanks and broke it, and gave it to them, saying, "This is my body given for you; do this in remembrance of me." Luke 22:19 (NIV)

THE WAY THE STORY ENDS

Sometimes a couple whose wedding I am officiating picks this verse to read during the ceremony: *"Place me like a seal over your heart, like a seal on your arm; for love is as strong as death, its jealousy unyielding as the grave. It burns like blazing fire, like a mighty flame. Many waters cannot quench love; rivers cannot sweep it away"* (Song of Songs 8:6-7 NIV).

Nothing is going to stop the king of glory from completing his story. Jesus is coming to rescue his bride. Jesus is going to make everything new! God promises life with him beyond the grave. A life where there will be no more death, mourning, crying, or pain. No more regrets, no more broken relationships, no more broken hearts.

When we realize that our story does not end in death but in life, we will deal with hardship differently. When we see our life as a story and not a perfect picture, suffering is not a chapter to be eliminated. Suffering is part of the bigger story of the "with me" God. If you're in a hard place, the cross tells us that Jesus understands and that not one ounce of your pain or your tears will be wasted. The Bible says, *"A bruised reed he will not break, and a smoldering wick he will not snuff out"* (Matthew 12:20).

God shoulders our weakness, and his strength becomes our own. He is making everything new. Clothing us in white, bringing beauty from ashes, for he will have his bride. Free from all her guilt and shame and known by her true name. Sons and daughters of the living God.

That's why we sing on Easter, because everything sad will become untrue. Our story will not end in death but in life. It will not end in a grave but in glory. It will end with a wedding feast. Dancing in the streets with joy in our hearts and with the people we love.

EASTER PEOPLE

Barbara Johnson said that we're Easter people, living in a Good Friday world. This is true every time we love. Every time a broken relationship is reconciled. Every time we hear cancer is in remission or someone says, "I will stay with you if things stay hard." We are Easter people living in a Good Friday world.

Every time we see the wings of the dawn over blue ocean waters. Every time we watch the sun descend in multicolors behind mountains of green. Every time we see hints of heaven on earth. We are Easter people in a Good Friday world.

Every time we laugh or eat a good meal. Every time we say "I'm sorry" from the heart. Every time man's best friend greets us at the door. We are Easter people living in a Good Friday world.

You may read this with uncertainty about the future or with sadness in your heart. You may be ready to move to a new job, but that is away from friends you love. You may hope beyond all hope that God will rise in your heart again and that you might hear his voice as clearly as a friend sitting next to you. You are Easter people living in a Good Friday world.

There is more for us. There is more for you. Look at his hands and see his side. He knows your suffering and sorrow, and your scars can be healed. The tomb is empty. Hope is alive. You can be Easter people in a Good Friday world.

EASTER

RING THE BELLS

Easter is about revival and courage. Easter is light defeating darkness and love rolling away the stone, whatever that stone may be. In our culture, Christmas seems to get all the pomp and circumstance, but Easter is why we have hope.

Easter is about raising our voices to sing, "Christ the Lord is risen today." Leonard Cohen, best known for his song "Hallelujah," wrote a line in another song that sounds like Easter to me. "Ring the bells that still can ring."

It feels like we have been living in difficult days for a long time, but Easter means we can ring the bells that still can ring.

We can ring the bells of hope for those who grieve because there is eternal life. We can ring the bells for those sitting in darkness. We can ring loud enough until a crack appears where the light gets in. We can ring the bells of justice for the oppressed because Jesus bled for justice and mercy. We can ring the bells around a meal with friends because that's where love is served.

We can ring the bells of spring when daffodils break through the dark soil and reach for the sun. We can ring the bells that wake up the church and say there is grace and beauty for those who feel like giving up. We can ring the bells that still can ring and offer the worn and weary a garment of praise instead of a spirit of despair.

Death or discouragement will never defeat Easter people. Jesus is risen, and he's not going anywhere. *"The punishment that brought us peace was on him, and by his wounds we are healed"* (Isaiah 53:5 NIV).

Ring the bells that still can ring. Jesus is risen, he is risen indeed.

CIRCLE OF THANKS

Who do you do life with? Let me explain. If you throw a rock in a pond on a calm day, who are the people that form the circles around you?

I'm not sure my pond is big enough to hold all the thanks needed for this book. Let me start with the original team of six who made this all possible.

To Mary Smith who listened to me when I wasn't sure how to turn a phrase. She would suggest a small change here and there to capture my thoughts while making sure I crossed all my t's and dotted all my i's. Thank you to Steve Smith, Mary's husband and an author in his own right. Steve helped me understand the complexities of publishing and what it would take to make a book. To Kelly Pious, our Managing Director at Hope Church, who graciously reminded me to keep writing, keep editing, and keep pressing on. To Jake Roth and our communications team. Your excitement for this project rubbed off on me. Thank you to Megan Buchan, a good friend and voracious reader who helped me in the early days of this devotional to get it right. Thank you to my administrative assistant Julie Lane. She has been with me for five years now and volunteered to be my book manager to keep all the pieces together. Julie has become a good friend and a quiet prayer warrior, praying for the mess that is me.

Thank you to Drew and Paige Daniels, who, several years ago, secretly recorded my staff devotions and had them transcribed into a little booklet called "The Great Before." They believed in the potential for something more.

Thank you to David Dwight. We have known each other as colleagues and friends for almost as long as I've been married to my wife. It can be none other than God's hand that our partnership in this Gospel work has lasted for over thirty years. We began working together in earnest through a weekly prayer meeting that started in a small office we called "the cave." David has always believed in me and given me fuel for the fire to write. Love you brother.

To the staff at Hope Church. These incredible and gifted people are more than co-workers; they are my friends. I can't believe I get to do this beautiful kingdom work with you.

Thank you to Nicole Unice. She is a gifted writer, pastor, and friend. In the early days, she told me that I had something worth saying. Thank you for believing in me and for inspiring me to keep writing. Jesus is still with us after we say amen.

To the people of Hope Church, that is who you are: "The People." You are the church. Your belief and your stories of faith, even when facing the headwinds of the hard, have inspired many of these devotions and given them life. For the students at HOPE, thanks for helping me avoid e-mails and inviting me into conversations with you in the Hope Café. You keep me young.

Finally, to my friends and family. To my good friend Chris Handley in Florence, South Carolina. You are the friend who sticks closer than a brother. Our families have grown up together. In my make-up and mess-ups, you have always prayed for me. To Dave Johnson, Keith Evans, and J.G. Carter, who put up with my sarcasm and brought laughter to my life. I hope some of these devotions make you smile.

If tears were the watermark on this page of thanks, they are welling up in me when my family comes to mind. I haven't always been there during the busy seasons of ministry. One of my oldest friends, the Apostle Paul, said this: *"I pray that you would know how wide and long and high and deep is the love of Christ."* One of the ways Jesus has demonstrated this love for me is time around the table with my family for a meal. I could travel far and wide but my children and grandchildren have already filled my bucket list.

To my wife Meg. There's an old line in a movie: "You complete me." Your love for me has done more than that. You have always pointed me to Jesus who makes me whole. You have held our family together over the years and you have held me. You always remind me of possibility and to take one season at a time. We have made a messy, beautiful life together. It's full of laughter, love, and lots of broken things. I wouldn't have it any other way.

Finally, to my Lord and Savior, Jesus Christ. His body was broken for me, and his blood was shed for me. It is by grace that I have been saved, and Jesus is pretty busy saving me every day. Most of these devotions have come out of my morning time on the front porch with my Lord. They are the result of his grace and inspiration. His word became flesh to me.

This is my circle of thanks, the concentric circles in my pond that have gently and humbly moved me closer to Jesus. I will be forever grateful.

– Pete

REFERENCES

Augustine of Hippo. *Confessions*. Translated by Maria Boulding. Hyde Park, NY: New City Press, 1997.

Bennett, Arthur, ed. "To Be Fit for God," from *The Valley of Vision: A Collection of Puritan Prayers & Devotions*. Edinburgh, Scotland: Banner of Truth Trust, 1975.

Bennett, Arthur, ed. *The Valley of Vision: A Collection of Puritan Prayers & Devotions*. Edinburgh, Scotland: Banner of Truth Trust, 1975.

Brown, Gregory. *Ephesians: Understanding God's Purpose for the Church (The Bible Teacher's Guide)*. BTG Publishing, 2016.

Bruner, Frederick Dale. *The Christbook: A Historical/Theological Commentary: Matthew 1-12*. Ann Arbor, MI: University of Michigan Press, 1987.

Buechner, Frederick. "Come and See," from *Secrets in the Dark: A Life in Sermons*. New York: HarperCollins, 2007.

Buechner, Frederick. "The Face in the Sky," in *The Hungering Dark*. New York: HarperOne, 1985.

Buechner, Frederick. "The Seeing Heart," from *Secrets in the Dark: A Life in Sermons*. New York: HarperCollins, 2007.

Buechner, Frederick. *Secrets in the Dark: A Life in Sermons*. New York: HarperCollins, 2007.

Buechner, Frederick. *The Clown in the Belfry: Writings on Faith and Fiction*. New York: HarperCollins Publishers, 1992.

Chambers, Oswald. "Justification by Faith," from *My Utmost for His Highest*. New York: Dodd, Mead & Co., 1935.

Chambers, Oswald. *My Utmost for His Highest*. New York: Dodd, Mead & Co., 1935.

Collier, Winn. *Love Big, Be Well: Letters to a Small-Town Church*. Grand Rapids, MI: William B. Eerdmans Publishing Company, 2017.

Eldredge, John. *Resilient: Restoring Your Weary Soul in These Turbulent Times*. Nashville, TN: Thomas Nelson Publishers, 2022.

Gire, Ken. *The Weathering Grace of God: The Beauty God Brings from Life's Upheavals*. Ann Arbor, MI: Servant Publications, 2001.

Jones, Sally Lloyd. *The Jesus Storybook Bible*. Grand Rapids, MI: Zonderkidz, 2007.

Keller, Tim. "Generous Justice (Lecture)." TheGospelCoalition.org, April 15, 2011.

Keller, Timothy. *Walking with God through Pain and Suffering*. New York: Viking Press, 2013.

Lewis, C.S. *Letters to Malcolm: Chiefly on Prayer.* New York: Mariner Books, 2002.

Lewis, C.S. *The Lion, the Witch, and the Wardrobe.* London, England: Geoffrey Bles, 1950.

Lewis, C.S. *The Silver Chair.* London, England: Geoffrey Bles, 1953.

Lewis, C.S. *The Weight of Glory.* New York: HarperOne, 2001.

Lucado, Max. *Grace: More Than We Deserve, Greater Than We Imagine.* Nashville, TN: Thomas Nelson Publishers, 2014.

Morris, Leon. *The Gospel According to John: The New International Commentary on the New Testament.* Grand Rapids, MI: William B. Eerdmans Publishing Company, 1995.

Nouwen, Henri J.M. *Our Light and Our Salvation: Advent Reflections.* Fenton, MO: Creative Communications for the Parish, 2004.

Nouwen, Henri. *Out of Solitude: Three Meditations on the Christian Life.* Notre Dame, IN: Ave Maria Press, 2004.

Ortberg, John. *Eternity Is Now in Session: A Radical Rediscovery of What Jesus Really Taught About Salvation, Eternity, and Getting to the Good Place.* Chicago, IL: Tyndale House, 2018.

Ortberg, John. *I'd Like You More If You Were More Like Me: Getting Real About Getting Close.* Chicago, IL: Tyndale Refresh, 2017.

Ortlund, Dane C. *Deeper: Real Change for Real Sinners.* Wheaton, IL: Crossway, 2021.

Ortlund, Dane. *Gentle and Lowly: The Heart of Christ for Sinners and Sufferers.* Wheaton, IL: Crossway, 2020.

Piper, John. "Grace for the New Year," from *Taste and See: Savoring the Supremacy of God in All of Life.* Colorado Springs, CO: Multnomah, 2016.

Powlison, David. *Take Heart: Daily Devotions to Deepen Your Faith.* Greensboro, NC: New Growth Press, 2022.

Sauls, Scott. *A Gentle Answer: Our "Secret Weapon" in an Age of Us Against Them.* TN: Thomas Nelson Publishers, 2020.

Stanley, Andy. "Nothing Divides Like Politics." August 29, 2020. https://your move.is/videos/nothing-divides-like-politics/

Stott, John. *The Cross of Christ.* Westmont, IL: InterVarsity Press, 1989.

Tripp, Paul David. *Journey to the Cross: A 40-Day Lenten Devotional.* Wheaton, IL: Crossway, 2021.

Warren, Tish Harrison. *Prayer in the Night: For Those Who Work or Watch or Weep.* Westmont, IL: InterVarsity Press, 2021.

Webster, Douglas. *In Debt to Christ: A Study in the Meaning of the Cross.* Jacksonville, FL: Highway Press, 1957.

ABOUT THE AUTHOR

Pete Bowell has served as Senior Associate and Co-founding Pastor of Hope Church in Richmond, Virginia, for 28 years. He is married to Meg. They have three grown children, and he is proud "Poppy" to three grandchildren. He is saved by grace.